AF593494

MOUSEWIVES & MUFFINTOPS

BUZZ WORDS & EUPHEMISMS
What They Really Mean

By S. J. Hartland

Acknowledgements

Thank you to the worldwide web, friends and family for their invaluable help with research.

For my girls, Rosie and Caitlin

ISBN 978 1903056 33 2

First published in the UK in 2009 by
Brown Dog Books
Bath BA2 3LR

Designed by Julia King
Illustrations by Del Thorpe

Produced in the UK

Printed in Malta by Gutenberg Press,
using vegetable oil-based inks.
The paper comprises 100% virgin fibre.
Pulps used are totally chlorine-free.

Contents

Do You Call a Spade a Spade?

Or is it an ergonomic excavating device?

This collection offers a fascinating and eclectic mix of buzz words, euphemisms, dysphemisms, doublespeak and circumlocutions. It exposes expressions which are used to soften a harsh truth or to introduce a note of mischievous malice. Ordinary and inconvenient facts may be disguised or veiled which serves to confuse and bewilder and, more often than not, that is the intention!

The collection offers both a wry ramble through the comical and sometimes blatantly ridiculous 'lace curtains' of English language, but doesn't forget the more sombre and serious ways in which language can be misused.

Never again be lost for a witty one-liner or caustic comment with categories to cover a multitude of different occasions.

Buzz words ~ trendy phrases or words

Euphemism ~ use of a word or phrase that is less offensive than another

Dysphemism ~ substitution of a harsh expression for a more neutral one

Doublespeak ~ ambiguous language intended to deceive or confuse

Circumlocution ~ a roundabout way of expressing something

'I think the expression "It's a small world" is really a euphemism for, "I keep running into people I can't stand".'

Brock Cohen

Occupations

'If I had to live my life over again, I'd be a plumber'

Albert Einstein

Title inflation or up-titling is a very simple way of giving employees a boost and a sense of importance without the need to pay them any more – so is often popular with management. The resulting titles can sound pretty impressive if not a little outlandish at times!

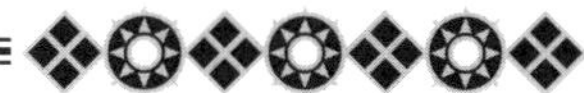

THE OFFICE

Administrative assistant

'The aspiring administrative assistant should be more than computer literate as much of this type of work is done on the computer.'

(directorym.co.uk)

Human Resources

'Human resource management (HRM) is a relatively modern label for the range of themes and practices involved in managing people.'

(HRM Guide)

Number cruncher

'Those with a real gift for figures are increasingly taking a central role in government at all levels. It's the revenge of the number crunchers.'

(The Independent)

Travel Management Consultant

Travel agent

Head of Verbal Communication

Business Development Assistant

Receptionist

Phone basher

'Do you have telesales experience? Are you a phone basher who is not afraid to make those cold calls?'

(liptonfleming.co.uk)

City slicker

'The weekly 12-part series follows six devoted slickers as they swap their fast-paced metropolitan lives for a crash course in Scottish country living.'

(entertainment.stv.tv)

Meteorologist

'Many may think that predicting the weather is the extent of what a meteorologist does. However, there are other applications for meteorology.'

(directorym.co.uk)

THE GLAMOUR WORLD

Visagiste

Make-up assistant

Facialist

'The facialist face-off:
One massages the faces of the stars in London, the other gets them red-carpet-ready in L.A. So what differentiates the top British and American facialists?'

(Style Magazine)

Booth babe or Booth bunny

'Tokyo Motor Show: Models of a different sort
This year's standouts from last week's show were the girls gracing the Ferrari and Maserati stand.'

(Tokyo Motor Show)

Exotic dancer

"They crossed the final frontier and the art went downhill," wrote exotic dancer historian, Jessica Grasscock in her book Striptease: "Strippers are completely naked now and that doesn't leave much to build an act around."

(insidebayarea.com)

Glamour model

'In recent years the glamour industry – once the undisputed province of the "page 3 model" – has now been accepted by the more mainstream media due to the rise of the "lad's mags" or "mid-shelf magazines".'

(purestorm.com)

CASUAL WORKERS

Office Cleaning Operative

Office cleaner

Victualler's assistant

Barmaid

Floor technician or **Domestic assistant**

'At the halls I lived in last year the cleaners were called "Domestic Assistants" despite the job involving nothing more than cleaning.'

Loss Prevention Officer

'If you're in the business of loss prevention, I'm sure you find yourself, from time to time, eyeing potential thieves in stores, on your days off.'

(rlpx.com)

Street Orderly

Road sweeper

Utensil Maintenance Person

Dishwasher

Vision Clearance Engineer

Transparent Wall Maintenance Officer

Window cleaner

Squeegee Merchant

'A London politician has called on the government to expunge "the menace of squeegee merchants" who clean car windshields at traffic lights without asking the permission of drivers.'

(moderncarcare.com)

POST OFFICE

Postal Worker

Mail Carrier

Delivery Officer

Postman

Despatch-room Facilitator

Post room clerk

SCHOOL

School Meals Supervisory Assistant

Lunchtime Supervisor

'Those claims were backed by lunchtime supervisor, Amanda Connellan who said: "Dinner times are a chance for the children to sit down together with their friends and have an enjoyable and healthy lunch."

(rochdaleonline.co.uk)

Educational Welfare Manager

Truancy Officer

Nitty Nora

'Bring back "Nitty Nora" – the children are always catching nits from school.'

THE HIGH STREET

Retail Representative

Sales Associate

'Sales Associate is nothing more than a fancy title for cashier or sales clerk. I have owned several businesses, current one for 30 years and it seems no one wants to work unless they have a "Title" for the position.'

(answers.yahoo.com)

Merchandiser

Ambient Replenishment Officer

Shelf stacker (as advertised in a Safeway recruitment advertisement in 1990s).

Nail Technician

'Sit back and relax in comfortable surroundings and be pampered by our friendly staff. Kookoo's professional nail technicians are ready to spoil you.....whether you need a simple manicure or a more intensive nail spa treatment...'

(kookoonails.com)

Colour Technician

'Colouring technician Kirsty Gorman, layered Carol's hair with a selection of warm caramel and soft browns with a few golden highlights to create a natural, softer colour.'

(Huddersfield Daily Examiner)

Turf Accountant

'Bookies at ease as gambling fraudster is behind bars
The nation's turf accountants breathed a sigh of relief yesterday as police revealed that a smooth-talking Liverpudlian known as "Pencil Man" had been arrested and placed under lock and key.'

(independent.co.uk)

Barista

'In essence a barista is someone who doesn't just make coffee – instead, to them, coffee making is an art.'

(communityfood.com)

Mixologist

'If you thought a mixologist was just a fancy term for a bartender you'd only be partially correct. A mixologist is more like a chef, creating new drinks, not just pouring them.'

(slashfood.com)

COUNCIL WORKERS

Refuse Collector
Sanitation Engineer
Environmental Engineer

Dustbin man

Canine Control Officer

Dog catcher

Vermin Control
Exterminating Engineer
Rodent Officer

'A pied piper is needed now more than ever before, as the country's rat population rises dramatically and rodent officers are kept constantly busy.'

(caterersearch.com)

Technical Horticultural Maintenance Officer

Gardener

IT PERSONNEL

Propeller head

'There's a respect for the guy who didn't upgrade his computer systems just because some propeller head told him it would "be cool to do it".'

(Business Week)

A geek

A point-dexter

A nerd

'He wasn't at all the goofy nerd people thought he was.'
(Candy Randall)

An alpha geek

'As part of our continuing coverage of Macworld Expo 2009, we hopped on the bus along with about 30 other alpha geeks to visit the Mecca of Macdom and pick up some Apple swag at the company store.'
(Túaw)

A mouse potato

'Small-business owners and managers, already tethered to their computers for long periods, are turning into "mouse potatoes", increasingly eating and working while on their computers and while online.'
(informationweek.com)

'Hard work never killed anybody but why take a chance?'
Edgar Bergen

THE POLICE

There are numerous assorted terms for the police; some are decidedly harsh while others are undeniably more compassionate.

Law Enforcement Officer

Peace Officer

Plods

Pigs

Copper

'Come back coppers!
Will a new ad campaign lure British bobbies back from Oz?
Many UK policemen have opted for a sunnier life "Down Under" but will they be swayed by a new Aussie ad campaign that launches next week, calling on expat officers to return home?'

(homesworldwide.co.uk)

Bobby

'Put more bobbies on the street, make Britain a safer place.'

Bizzies

Liverpool slang

Rozzers

'So the rozzers stopped us to see if we were terrorists, obviously we said we were.'

(Motorcycle News)

The fuzz

'Caught By The Fuzz' by Supergrass
This is about lead singer, Gaz Coombs being caught in possession of cannabis when he was 15.'

(songfacts.com)

AND FINALLY...

Not forgetting the following, which although they fall outside the previous categories, definitely deserve a mention.

Head shunter

Reverse of head hunter, hired to get employees to leave and therefore avoid a costly redundancy package.

Domestic engineer

'My Mum doesn't work in an office, she's a domestic engineer. Domestic engineers don't get enough credit for all the work they do in the house.'

(Urban Dictionary)

Mousewife

Housewife spending her free time on the internet

Headshrinker or shrink

Psychiatrist

Collection correspondent

Debt collector

Liquid re-coating specialist

Painter and decorator

Shock Jock

'Roche and others from the new wave of women shock-jocks tell us that baring their fantasies or recounting their love lives in lurid and exhaustive detail is uniquely emancipating.'

(dailymail.co.uk)

Equine chiropodist

'Craigsteel's Amazing Feet
Henry Cecil advertised his skills as an equine chiropodist as Craigsteel broke the track record to win the Group Two Princess of Wales's Green King Stakes on the opening day of Newmarket's July meeting yesterday.'

(The Irish Times)

Factory farming

Large scale intensive farming focused on profit not welfare of animals

Boutique farmer

"Those boutique dairies are the wave of the future," said Kelly Smith, executive director of the S. C. Dairy Association. "It's a way for the small and medium sized milk farmers to increase income by appealing to customers' preference for locally grown food."

(greenvilleonline.com)

People

'No one can be exactly like me.
Sometimes even I have trouble doing it.'

Tallulah Bankhead

Are you a 'Fashionista', a 'Yummy Mummy', a 'Wild Child' or simply outgoing? In today's world where everyone needs a label it's just not enough to be simply yourself. So glance at the following categories and choose your own moniker – be the person you always wanted to be.

PERSONALITIES

A colourful past

'Colourful past threatens Giuliani's lead
His current advisors fear that his colourful past and his liberal social positions could scupper his candidacy.'

(freerepublic.com)

A free spirit

Rebel, non-conformist

A carrot cruncher

Someone from rural surroundings

Uninhibited

Very few social skills

Edgy

'Keys steps in to deliver edgy presence
Whether it's her "New Yawk" accent, her old school R&B flavour or even her swagger, Alicia Keys has an edgy presence – and then there's her booming voice.'

(theage.com.au)

Green welly brigade

'To the delight of countryside campaigners everywhere, former SkyNews autocutie Selina Scott is firmly establishing herself as the proud pin-up for the impassioned Green Welly Brigade.'

(findarticles.com)

Mess-mongers

'So, you've been talked into going to the beach for the day with your friends. And these friends – although you really like them and enjoy spending time with them – are of the messier variety. Here's what you'll need to safeguard yourself and your car from the mess-mongers: a couple of plastic bags… Oh, who are we kidding? Take a box of plastic bags. These will come in handy when your friends are about to throw their sopping wet suits onto the seats of your car.'

(thecampuschronicle.com)

Bubbly

"TV is a possibility", she says, describing herself as "a proper chatterbox."

"I love being in front of the camera but I've got such a loud, bubbly personality that I think I need to be shouting my mouth off."

(Liverpool Echo)

Outgoing

Gregarious

Loud

Life of the party

Louder still…

Substance dependent

"This isn't a life," the substance dependent, alarmingly withered singer tearfully acknowledged.'

(music.msn.com of Amy Winehouse)

Stress puppy

Someone who thrives on stress

Hippy dippy

'Paltrow sheds "hippy dippy" chrysalis:
Teetering in seven inch heels and in a barely there black dress, actress Gwyneth Paltrow shrugged off her earth mother image yesterday at the London Premiere of her latest film.'

(The Australian)

Hobo chic

'…worn boyfriend jeans with leather suspenders hanging down below the hip, patched leggings and other battered looks that were shocking for their lack of finish and still quite cool. Like we said, hobo chic.'

(newsday.com)

Paparazzi fodder

'Posh'n'Becks, meanwhile, are paparazzi fodder; cut-out dolls, flaunting themselves for the flashbulbs in a knowingly selected his'n'hers range of designer outfits.'

(thisislondon.co.uk)

Spontaneous

Scatter-brain

The blogger

'Mum's hooked on blogging
The "blog" – an online commentary or diary – has long been a popular tool with politicians and others keen to express their opinions to a wider audience but a new class of person is increasingly becoming hooked on it as a relaxation aid – mothers.'

(walesonline.co.uk)

Workaholic

'Very often women workaholics forego sleep, because they've bought into the mentality that says sleep time is unproductive time. Yet what have all this workaholism and sleep loss bought us?'

(independent.com.mt)

A numpty

'A trucker dubbed "numpty" and "thicky" by workmates has been offered a place at Cambridge University.'

(mirror.co.uk)

Pain in the bum

Pain in the neck

'Shadow Minister for Transport, Robert Goodwill said: "Rogue wheel clampers are a pain in the neck for drivers up and down the country."

(thisishullandeastriding.co.uk)

APPEARANCE

Swarthy

'He had grime under his fingernails and looked like he was allergic to bathtubs and showers because the accumulated dirt on his skin gave him a swarthy look.'

(thenorthwestern.com)

A salad dodger

Overweight person who shuns fruit and vegetables

Exotic

'Singer and actress Eartha Kitt, whose exotic sex-kitten persona and sultry purring vocal delivery was unlike anything that had come before her.'

(flickr.com)

Tanorexic

'Beauty queen almost "tanned herself to death" because of sunbed addiction'

(telegraph.co.uk)

Bee-stung lips

'Ever since Angelina Jolie became the ultimate sex-symbol, every woman's fantasy has been to have full, pouty lips.'

(inoutstar.com)

A chrome dome

'The old chrome dome told me that grass doesn't grow where there is a lot going on'.

(alphadictionary.com)

Follicularly challenged

"Poor Alopecia – was her father follicularly challenged?"

A high forehead
Baldielocks
Lightbulb lookalike
Moby
Thin on top
Slaphead
Hair needy

Bald or balding

Metal mouth
Brace face

'Brace face cool
With tiny wires, choices of colourful bands or nearly invisible brackets, braces have gone fashion forward.'

(djournal.com)

Less favoured by beauty
Swamp donkey

Ugly

Jug lugs

Large protruding ears

Vertically challenged

'It's a new era at Disney. From now on "Snow White and the Seven Dwarfs" will be known as "Person of No Colour and the Seven Vertically Challenged Individuals."

(quotesdaddy.com)

THE HOI POLLOI

A displaced worker

Unemployed

A down and out

A vagrant

A crusty

A pavement person

Homeless person, beggar

A traveller

A pikey

A gypsy

Litter lout

'One in five drivers regularly tosses litter out of the car window'

(autoexpress.co.uk)

Cowboy

'Cowboy builders are trying to rip off thousands of flood victims, the Government warned yesterday.'

(mirror.co.uk)

Rogue trader

'Police are warning people in the city about rogue traders after an elderly lady was conned at her home in Eaton.'

(eveningnews.24.co.uk)

A PG (paying guest)

'....the lodger was a symbol in middle class circles of dwindling finances, the shame of which was not alleviated even when he or she was referred to as a "paying guest."

(independent.co.uk)

A junkie

'Vanishing junkies worries

Drug addicts sent to Weston-super-Mare are vanishing after their treatment according to a West MP'

(Western Daily Press)

A chav

'The stereotypical image of a chav is an aggressive white teen or young adult of working class background who wears branded sports and casual clothing (baseball caps are also common) who often fights and engages in petty criminality and often assumed to be unemployed or in a low paid job.'

(englishopinion.today.com)

Stands for 'council house and violent'

Grazers

"Grazers" chew up store profits

Supermarkets estimate they are losing £207 million a year due to "grazers" who steal food and eat it in the aisles.'

(thesun.co.uk)

Scally

'Past attempts to shake off our image of scallies and shell suits

...the city still labours under the stereotypical image of a grim, battle-scarred centre of crime...'

(Liverpool Echo)

Benefit tourist

Foreigner coming to live in Britain off state benefits

Light fingered

'Light-fingered bibliophiles

The plot sounds like an ultra-British detective story. A collection of rare books initially valued at about $2 million, including a 1638 edition of Galileo's Discorsi, disappear from London's University College Library.'

(time.com)

Economically disadvantaged

Fiscal underachiever

Economically marginalised

Poor person

Vegitatum davenportae

A couch potato

'Dr Caroline Gamlin says that "couch potato culture" is costing lives and she is calling for people across the region to take advantage of the many opportunities for keeping active, that Somerset has to offer.'

(thisissomerset.co.uk)

GIRLS, GIRLS, GIRLS

A showflake

Unreliable female who doesn't keep appointments

Beach bunny

Devoted to lying on beach in the sun

PR bunny

'We've each been around long enough to have heard all the nonsense about "PR bunnies" (or "Fluffy bunnies" as I've heard them called in the UK) and we don't think anyone will confuse us as such. In fact, we did a straw poll and it seems the PR girl that Professor French describes – "images of vacuous little pretty girls as 'office dressing' and 'shuffled off' to perform clerical duties deemed to be beneath PR management, which is most often male" – is somewhat of an urban myth.'

(prgirlz.com)

Yummy Mummy

'The Yummy Mummy is a mother who juggles her career and party-girl lifestyle.'

(Harper's Bazaar)

Slummy Mummy

'A quick Amazon search for "Slummy Mummy" delivers dozens of recent women-only novels with titles such as The Undomestic Goddess, The Accidental Wife, The Playground Mafia and Secret Diary of a Demented Housewife to name a few. Who after all, wouldn't cheer for the underdog who burns the soufflé and drops the kids off to school in her dressing gown?'

(guardian.co.uk)

Prommies

'Meet the Prommies, or professional mummies, who, due to dwindling business, City cutbacks and lay-offs, now find themselves at home with a new job description: Mother.'

(Sunday Times Style)

It Girl

'Edie Sedgwick: The It girl who was inspiration to Dylan & Warhol
To some, she was just a society heiress who did a lot of drugs. But to Andy Warhol and Bob Dylan, Edie Sedgwick was a muse – a wild blonde superstar who defined the look and excesses of the Sixties.'

(independent.co.uk)

Glamourati

'At Egg this Saturday, the cream of club land can anticipate a line up they've only dreamt of, with unique surprises, a live element and a DJ line up that will leave London's glamourati begging for more.'

(blissout.blogspot.com)

Totty

'Astrid and sister Davina, classic posh totty from Chelsea-in-the-country acres of Wiltshire, are mates with Prince William's patient girlfriend "Waity Katy" Middleton.'

(blatherskite.com)

Crumpet

'She was the original "thinking man's crumpet" and remains disarmingly frank about sex.'

(dailymail.co.uk on Joan Bakewell)

A-listers

'The Oscars unveiled
Will Hollywood's "A-listers" opt for pared-back sober elegance on the Oscars red carpet this year, or will they go for all-out glamour? The fashion world remains undecided.'

(The Scotsman)

Bimbo

'University Challenge star divides opinion
Some viewers backed the contestant, with one writing: "I am on the side of those who find it rather attractive and a welcome change to the bimbo culture that the TV reality curse has spawned."

(digitalspy.co.uk)

Vivacious

'And whether she's sporting her dark and dangerous burlesque gear or a stunning platinum blonde wig, no-one can quite hit the spot like vivacious Vikki.'

(The Sun)

Bohemian

'Mischa Barton channels Axl
'She's definitely known for being bohemian and for her hippie look but then you will turn a page and see her in head-to-toe Chanel.'

(handbag.com)

Wild child

'Since becoming a mother, Nicole Ritchie insists her partying, wild child days are behind her.'

(dailymail.co.uk)

WAGs

Footballers' wives and girlfriends

Internal fashion victim

Has inner health obsessions, takes a lot of vitamins

Trophy wife

'A trophy wife often comes from a similar socio-economic background as her spouse but tends to play a more subservient role during public appearances.'

(wisegeek.com)

Eye candy or Arm candy

'The CIA was decorated lavishly for the occasion in new décor – a perfect setting for the bevy of "eye candy" models dressed in beautiful gowns.'

(St Helena Star)

Domestic goddess

'Mixing up some other foul-looking festive mess, the self-styled Domestic Goddess purred: "Now some butter…just a small amount." Small..?'

(Sunday Mirror)

Bit of fluff

'I'm not just Jim Davidson's bit of fluff…
Just because you're a hostess doesn't mean you are a brainless bimbo.'

(Sunday Mirror)

Bit of skirt

'Dear Jenny: He eyes up every bit of skirt
Something that really annoys me about my boyfriend, who I have been going out with for six years now, is the way he always eyes up other women.'

(getreading.co.uk)

Latest squeeze

'Orlando Bloom has set the dating rumour mill turning once again and his latest squeeze is said to be Bruce Willis' daughter, Rumer.'

(Marie Claire)

Ladette

'Growing ladette culture means young women who work in offices are twice as likely to drink themselves to death as the rest of the population.'

(alcoholpolicy.net)

MAINLY MEN

Lothario

'Kendra Wilkinson cheated on ex-boyfriend Hugh Hefner because she "had to have sex". The 23 year old star – who recently moved out of the Playboy mansion after splitting from the 82 year old lothario – admits she used to "sneak" out of the famous party house to get the satisfaction Hugh couldn't provide.'

(PerthNow Australia)

Tireless raconteur

'Sir Peter Richard Haydon 1913 – 1971
A "big and exuberant man" and an able public speaker, he was in private conversation a "splendid (and tireless) raconteur."

(adb.online.anu.edu.au)

For this read, unstoppable bore

A bon viveur

'A noted bon viveur he had a passion for French cuisine'

(idioms.thefreedictionary.com)

Ideas hamster

'Bob Geldof: From Boomtown Rat to ad agency "idea hamster"

"He says he'll be working with "ideas hamsters" – people with creative minds who are constantly churning out new ideas.'

(The Independent)

A boffin

'University boffin knighted

A Manchester University professor, who is one of the country's top experts in pure mathematics, has been knighted for lifelong services to science.'

(Manchester Evening News)

White collar workers

'Recession hits "white collar" staff

White collar staff in management and consulting have been the biggest victims of the recession so far, new figures showed.'

(The Press Association)

A chinless wonder

'They are to do with allegations that he is a chinless wonder, an upper class twit, the Little Lord Fauntleroy of Notting Hill.'

(mirror.co.uk)

Beefcake

"Lost" beefcake wouldn't wish his supreme looks, fame on anyone
Josh Holloway's Sawyer character on "Lost" is the perfect mix of hot. He's a bad boy with a sensitive side, and thanks to the island climate, he's generally shirtless.'

(popeater.com)

A hunk

'Scrummy Hunks
The sporting hunks stripped off their kit to reveal their muscles and their fantastic ball-handling skills.'

(dailystar.co.uk)

Stud muffin

'Then, to further prove what a manly, woman-loving, heterosexual, stud muffin he is, Chesney talks about the "long line of girls" that he has had sex with.'

(babble.com.au)

A ladies' man

'He's also a tremendous gossip, a perceptive analyst of other people and quite a ladies' man. His memoirs cannot help but be entertaining.'

(entertainmenttimesonline.co.uk on Robert Wagner)

Alfresco urinators

Men who urinate outdoors

Middle youth or **Peter Pan men**

'Media reports have focused on the "Peter Pan Syndrome" – the growing phenomenon of young men who don't seem to want to grow up. They drift from job to job, live with parents or with a crew of buddies and focus much of their energy on drinking, carousing, watching sports, playing video games and chasing women.'

(familylifeculturewatch.com)

Alpha male

'They've got all the elements of a quintessential Mills & Boon romance; jet set locations, hunky alpha male heroes and hot sex.'

(telegraph co.uk)

Beta male

'Dearest D. H.
Your girlfriend doesn't recognise a good Beta Male when she has one. Females who have the lion's chunk of earning power need to take care of their supportive men folks the same way men used to provide for our vacuum-cleaning asses in less enlightened times.'

(sfgate.com)

Beach bum

A devotee of the beach

Bambi

'Born Again Middle-Aged Biker
There's a new breed of easy rider on the roads. Born-again bikers are hitting 40 and rediscovering a passion for speed, leathers and powerful motorcycles.'

(independent.co.uk)

Adrenaline junkie or Base jumper

'Base jumpers are what psychologists call "high-sensation seekers", people who need regular dopamine and adrenaline hits in order to feel satisfied.'

(Sunday Times Magazine)

Unhinged

'Unhinged Sean loses the plot when he finds out the truth about little Amy's paternity on Christmas Day, and he kidnaps the tot, taking her to a dingy squat.'

(The Sun)

Odorously challenged

Sweaty

Smuggling grapes

Male wearing his Speedo swimming trunks with pride

FOLLOWERS OF FASHION

A fashion guru

'London Fashion Week:
Make sure you are looking hot this season with advice from top stylists and fashion gurus'

(itvlocal.com)

Fashionista

'Victoria Beckham: I lie in bed thinking about what to wear
Victoria 34, says she was destined to become a fashionista. "I was never that good a singer but I think I am good at fashion"

(Now Magazine)

Fashion victim

Someone who follows every fashion trend

Fashion roadkill

An unsuccessful follower of fashion

Recessionista

'Debenhams reported a surge of its own designer range – a trend put down to a new type of shopper it called "the recessionista", who opts for equivalents to expensive labels.'

(Daily Mail)

Shopaholic

'Art matters: Confessions of a Shopaholic
Anyway, the plot is this: Isla Fisher plays Rebecca, a shopping junkie, who writes, inappropriately, for a New York financial advice magazine. Unrequited love, fabulous clothes and debt build up.'

(entertainment.timesonline.co.uk)

Mutton dressed as lamb

Woman dressing younger than is appropriate for her age

Coolth

At the absolute height of fashion

THE PLANET'S LESS FORTUNATE

'Just like a pair of children's scissors, bright and colourful but not too sharp'.

Unknown

The following phrases may produce a guilty grin if picturing a colleague or friend but they are not intended to cause offence, so please use sparingly and with caution at all times!

Six ants short of a picnic

His belt doesn't go through all the loops

Has a room temperature IQ

You're too slow to catch a cold

As quick as a tree

'He really is rather slow mentally, I don't mean to be cruel but he's just about as quick as a tree.'

His porch light is on but there is nobody home

He wasn't strapped in during launch

His grey matter doesn't matter

Couldn't count water in a bucket

Skating on the wrong side of the ice

All crown and no filling

As useful as Bolognese sauce on shoelaces

Can't find his couch in the living room

Couldn't hit sand if he fell off a camel

Brain's on cruise control

He couldn't organise his way out of a paper bag

'It's liable to be a dog-eat-dog fight for the London Mayoral Election and it really is down to Boris vs. Ken. Boris must realise that some people may have spotted he couldn't organise his way out of a paper bag.'

(blog@wordpress.com)

He should have sold when his IQ reached 29

Full throttle, dry tank

She's booked out of Grey Matter Motel

One pancake short of a stack

Out of his depth in a puddle

'We had sausage and mash which consisted of lumpy mash and cheap under-cooked pork sausages. The previous reviewer who made the hilarious comment about the new manager being "out of his depth in a puddle" was absolutely right.'

(london-eating.co.uk)

I'm having a stupid attack

'I can't believe I've done that already, I'm having a stupid attack.'

Sharp as a doughnut

One bean short of a chilli

He's half a bubble off plumb

Gives short planks a bad name

'He's the type of student that gives short planks a bad name. The only thing that surprised me was that he made it to second year of a university course.'

As quick as a corpse

He looks for the 'ANY' key

Got a leak in his think tank

Bright as a night light

'Don has never been clever, in fact he's about as bright as a night light.'

A few birds shy of a flock

Cunning as a dodo

One sock short of a pair

He's only gargled from the fountain of knowledge

'I don't know how well he will do in his exams, he's not that clever, he's only ever gargled from the fountain of knowledge.'

As keen as a vegetable

A dim bulb in the marquee of life

There are some pages missing

'He means well and tries really hard but there are definitely some pages missing.'

The lights are flashing, the gate is down but the train isn't coming

Out to lunch

'There's no point in trying to explain it to him, he doesn't seem to take it in; he appears to be out to lunch most of the time.'

Lonely Hearts Column

'You can't buy love on Ebay'

Unknown

The personal advertisements that appear in magazines, newspapers or online usually contain a wealth of misleading and sycophantic language that requires a little translation ....

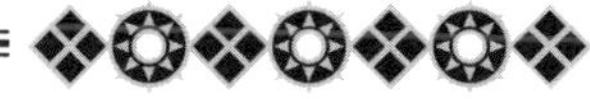

WOMEN SEEKING MEN

Likes to party

Could have an alcohol problem

Wild and outgoing

Gets drunk very easily

Happy, uncomplicated

Perhaps not the brightest button in the box?

Fun or Bubbly

'I am a happy bubbly lady who is very romantic and likes to receive flowers'
Annoying and spoilt

Young looking

Definitely middle aged

30 something

Realistically about 42

Artistic, vivacious brunette

Wears brightly coloured kaftans and likes to think of herself as an extrovert

Average looking

Ugly

Affectionate

'Jenny from Crewe, affectionate and looking for love.'
Needy

Looking for a snuggle buddy

Has a lot of soft toys and pink fluffy stuff

Beautiful

Spends too much time in front of the mirror

Rubenesque, curvaceous, voluptuous

Overweight

Headstrong

May be argumentative

Romantic

'Carrie, attractive brunette hoping for romantic evenings by the fire'.
Looks better in soft lighting

This cougar is looking for her prey

Definitely a man eater

Likes eating out

'Sue from Manchester area seeks professional man for meals out'
Probably lazy and overweight

A face carved by angels

*??**??*

MEN SEEKING WOMEN

Looking for a soul mate

Keep away, sounds like a stalker

Likes cuddles

Insecure, maybe looking for a mother figure?

Financially stable, well educated, charismatic, well travelled

'Peter well educated, enjoys culture and travel, hoping to find a like minded lady who enjoys the finer things in life.'
Arrogant and patronising

Uninhibited

Lacks any form of censorship

Possible relationship

Definitely looking for more than a friendship

Playmate

'John from Birmingham looking for playmate, adult fun, no strings relationship'
Really just wants sex

Young at heart

Could be a pensioner or certainly over 60

Nice looking with great body much younger than my age

Definitely 60 plus

Youthful

'Jason, youthful, slightly crazy with a zest for life, looking for someone to share adventures'
Late 40s- early 50s but thinks he can still wear hoodies

I am considered good looking and in my early fifties

..but really and truly, I am much older

GSOH

Good Sense of Humour – in other words likes juvenile pranks

Unpretentious

Boring

Widower with a zest for life

You have been warned

Flexible, open minded

Desperate

A switch hitter
Bi-guy
AC/DC
Ambidextrous
To swing both ways

'Lady Gaga swings both ways in new video
Lady Gaga turns on the raunch in her new music video by snogging both a boy and a girl.'

(metro.co.uk)

Sensitive

Gay and caring

Relationships

'Before I met my husband I'd never fallen in love, though I'd stepped in it a few times'

Rita Rudner

Starter marriage

Short-lived first marriage, ends in divorce with no children

Open marriage

Where both husband and wife indulge in extra-marital relationships

To shack-up

'Asking your girlfriend to move in with you seems like a good idea. It's the fantasy of waking up to freshly brewed coffee, hot waffles and clean matching socks that has you contemplating the big question: "To shack-up or not to shack-up?"

(thefrisky.com)

Liaison

'John Profumo, the former British minister whose liaison with a call girl, nearly brought down a government and who spent more than 40 years redeeming himself with unpaid work among London's poor, died after suffering a stroke, an official said Friday.'

(Dawn.com)

Fence jumping

Adultery

Petite amie or **Other woman**

'Anthea Turner's entire career fell to bits when she, too, became "the other woman" and "stole" Della Bovey's husband, Grant.'

(dailymail.co.uk)

Petit maison or **Love nest**

'The Petit Trianon nearby was built by Louis XV in 1763 as a love-nest for his long-term mistress Madame Pompadour.'

(smh.com.au)

A sugar daddy

'A friend who looks 34 but is in fact a 44-year-old single mother of two thumping teenagers, says she gets her "sugar daddy" to pay for her Botox.'

(women.timesonline.co.uk)

Gentleman friend or **lady friend**

A discreet way of referring to a partner in later life

Toy boy

'Madonna seems to be taking advantage of her new-found single status by hitting the town with yet another toy boy. Last night she was snapped with another male companion at the Waverley Inn in New York.'

(entertainmnetwise.com)

Cradle snatcher

A person in a relationship with someone much younger than themselves

To have grown apart

The relationship has come to an end

LATs (Living Alone Together)

'New research estimates that there are now as many as 2 million couples who, despite being in a committed relationship, live separately. The number of couples who live apart together (LATs) is now roughly the same as those who live under the same roof.'

(timesonline.co.uk)

SBLTs (Single But Living Together)

'Until recently, if a home owning couple had a major bust-up, the solution was relatively straightforward; split up, sell up and move on. Now however, the credit crunch and negative equity mean that couples simply can't afford to. Instead they're forced to continue living under the same roof and, in several instances, even share the same bed.'

(Telegraph Weekend)

Smoking bed

Evidence of sexual misconduct by a public figure

Commitment jewellery

Engagement ring

'Marriage is a wonderful invention: then again so is a bicycle repair kit'.

Billy Connolly

HANKY PANKY

'Sex without love is an empty experience, but as empty experiences go, it's one of the best.'

Woody Allen

That age old euphemism for, what people find too embarrassing to mention; sex. We would far rather prevaricate than be explicit, consequently the resulting number of euphemisms is long and varied; some mischievously amusing whilst others are simply smutty - there follows a select assortment.

Love life

'Glenda Jackson recounts a love life characterised by violence
"I don't think I have ever been in a relationship with a man in which he hasn't raised his fists to me."

(The Independent)

Getting jiggy

'We're all sensual beings and when it comes to getting jiggy with your partner of choice, it's nice to set the mood.'

(Irish independent)

A bit of slap and tickle

'I found myself on a warm beach with a not unattractive woman. We were both drunk and we went for it. Yes we did wrong – but neither of us could ever have dreamed that 5 minutes of slap and tickle would get us thrown in jail.'

(Thaindian News)

Having a fumble

The bedroom department

'X Factor mentor, Sinitta rates former boyfriend, Simon Cowell as "11 ¾ out of 10" in the bedroom department.'

(The Sun)

Bedroom gymnastics

'If asked "How was it for you darling?" Most women would probably respond "Not very interesting thank you!" The half term report for bedroom gymnastics class can be best summarised as "Must try harder".

(responsesource.com)

Ocean motion

Getting squelchy

To do the horizontal tango

Doing the horizontal hokey pokey

A roll in the hay

'Your child is as likely to hear about sex with pets, corpses or someone else's wife on prime time broadcast television as to see a happily married couple having a roll in the hay, according to a study by one of the self appointed watchdog groups.'

(washingtonpost.com)

Inserting tab 'A' into slot 'B'

Doing the 'no pants dance'

Going fishing for trouser trout

'Gail has been a trouser trout angler for 30 years. After a catch and release first marriage and 14 years of swimming and treading water, Gail landed her prize trophy trout in 2000.'

(lamasbeauty.com)

Wrinkly activity

Older generation having sex

Fertilizing the flower bed

Doing the twist and shout

Organ grinding

Making whoopee

'Tis the season for making whoopee
The Christmas–New Year's period produces a year–high spike in sexual activity and conceptions in the United States.'

(theworks.gather.com)

Rumpy-pumpy

'A survey has revealed money worries and unhappiness are contributing to a rumpy-pumpy slump with 28 per cent of people having less sex than this time last year.'

(dailyrecord.co.uk)

Being active

'She also called having sex "being active" which makes it sound like something an old person might do to keep the circulation going.'

(Irish Independent)

...not forgetting the long standing euphemism, originally used when barber shops sold condoms:

Something for the weekend sir?

'Now the phrase "something for the weekend sir?" is to make a comeback. The Government has told health workers to provide teenage boys with free condoms in barbers' shops.'

(independent.co.uk)

Private Parts...Naughty Bits... Nether Regions

'Men live in a fantasy world. I know this because I am one and I actually receive my mail there.'

Scott Adams

The greatest embarrassment, bar none, is talking about and naming the male and female genital organs and that's where euphemisms come in handy. Rather than cause any offence or embarrassment it's always safer to use a jokey or light-hearted reference thus avoiding the impossibly unmentionable.

MALE BITS

Crotch

'Flying without wings: life on a "crotch rocket"
Sometimes called a "crouch rocket" for its speed and the way the rider sits on the motorbike, the light-weight urban racer has found its market in small town America and the big city – even if its name does give pause.'

(tri-statedefenderonline.com)

Percy

John Thomas

Willy

'My son pushed his willy between his legs and pretended to be a girl.'

(thedailymash.co.uk)

One eyed trouser snake

One eyed zipper fish

Equipment

Wedding tackle

'Woman bites boyfriend in "wedding tackle"

A word of warning this fine autumn afternoon: Do not mess with 49 year-old Constance Marie Manning of Fort Wayne, Indiana, who is as far as we're aware still in Allen County lock up on a "felony count of criminal recklessness" and a misdemeanour count of "domestic battery". This follows her attacking her boyfriend with multiple weapons including a knife, a dog figurine and her laughing gear. Manning hit the poor chap with a dog figurine and "then began to bite him in the groin area."

(theregister.co.uk)

The wife's best friend

Performance weapon

Hot dog

FEMALE BITS

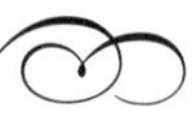

'Chanel No.5'

Marilyn Monroe, when asked what she wore in bed.

Kitty

Pussy

'Maybe you've heard of a little production called "The Vagina Monologues", a play in which pussy monsters are glorified in all sorts of terrible ways.'

(cornellsun.com)

Beaver

Front bottom

Fanny

'It's as if he's taken Johnny Craddock's infamous advice: "I hope all your doughnuts turn out like Fanny's"

(guardian.co.uk)

Quim

'What is it with today's young gels and their obsession with flashing shaved quim?'

(independent.co.uk)

Tush

'If Britney had flashed her tush and tits in Ibiza, no one would have given a monkeys.'

(independent.co.uk)

And then there are the page 3 model's greatest assets…

Bazookas

Bristols

Boobs

'Melinda Messenger has revealed that the Dancing on Ice ladies all perform a "boob test" before taking to the ice "We go behind this curtain and jump up and down just to make sure they don't spill out."

(entertainment.stv.tv)

Tits

Rack

Knockers

'Wayne Rooney's outrageous cousin has decided to increase her huge 34F knockers to a whopping 34J cup to become the girl with the largest chest in her home town.'

(clickliverpool.com)

Weapons of mass distraction

'An Easyjet ad displaying a pair of bikini-clad breasts beneath the phrase "Discover weapons of mass distraction" has escaped censure from the advertising watchdog despite 200 complaints.'

(brandrepublic.com)

Brothels

'You can lead a hor-ti-culture but you can't make her think.'

Dorothy Parker

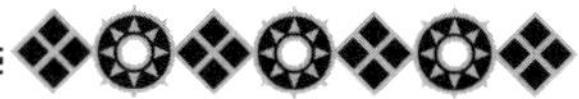

Red light district

'Some may see it as perverse but sex is often a tourist attraction. After all prostitution is the oldest game in town, a part of life; and red light districts definitely do regularly attract tourists.'

(Sydney Morning Herald)

House of profession

Massage parlour

'A massage parlour, whose website offers threesomes and steamy sex sessions, is under investigation by the town's police.'

(Loughborough Echo)

Naughty house
House of sin
House of pleasure
Bawdy house

House of ill repute

'Few archaeologists say that they specialize in studying houses of ill repute. Scientists usually stumble across brothels while looking for something more traditional like an elegant fountain or extension of an ancient road.'

(The Seattle Times)

Birdcage

'The ladies of the night or soiled doves, worked the customers of the Birdcage 24 hours a day. They plied their trade in cribs suspended from the ceiling. The ladies would close the drapes to entertain their clients with champagne, kisses and other favours of the trade.'

Knocking shop

'Little knocking shop of scripting horrors
Why pay for something you can get for free? That's a double barrelled question when it comes to "Satisfaction"- a pay-television drama series set in an upmarket Melbourne brothel called 232.'

(The Australian)

Hot-pillow hotel

Bordello

'This must be how men feel when they go to a high class bordello, I thought, and the madam parades her best girls for the client.'

(mvn.com)

Sauna parlour

'Indoor prostitution has always been more tolerated in Edinburgh but Glasgow City Council have been keen to clamp down on brothels, saunas and massage parlours.'

(DailyRecord.co.uk)

Escort agency

'Small ads for escort agencies, which play a pivotal role in the trial of a British woman accused of running a top-class international prostitution ring, were banished from its columns yesterday by the International Herald Tribune.'

(The Independent)

Hourly hotel

Skivvie-house

Sporting-house

Hot house

The Womanly Figure

'She had curves in places that other women don't even have places.'

Cybill Shepherd of Marilyn Monroe

One person's fat is another person's shapely just as one person's skinny is another's slender. The issue of weight is constantly in the media with pressure to conform to the 'perfect model-type figure' that only hours of working out at the gym and strict low-carb dieting can produce. Hence we seem to have acquired an ever increasing glossary of weight related phrases – some kinder than others.

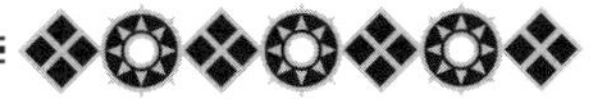

Curvaceous

A shapely woman

Spare tyre

Bingo wings

'My body has suddenly started to get a little bit softer. I don't want a belly and bingo wings so I've really got into the gym.'

(Denise Van Outen in fabulousmag.co.uk)

Chubby

Ample

Muffin top

'So these Valetta bound girls squeeze themselves into low-slung jeans which are obviously three sizes too small for them because, for some odd reason, their bodies have not grown in a Gina Lollobrigida way, but in that unforgiving flat-ass, muffin top belly, small pointy tits way that only a vengeful God and bags of crisps could concoct.'

(maltatoday.com)

Love handles

'An American cosmetic surgeon has gotten himself into a bit of trouble for his creative solution to rising fuel costs. Dr. Alan Bittner revealed on his website that he runs his 4WD on human fat removed during liposuction operations. His website continues, "Not only do they lose their love handles or chubby belly but they get to take part in saving the earth."'

(The Canberra Times, Australia)

Pleasantly plump

'Hairspray – a pleasantly plump musical and a pleasantly plump teenager bring new life to feature films.'

(channel24.co.za)

The fuller figure

'Size is a big issue for people with full figures and it is important to make sure that you buy clothes that do fit you. Don't try and squeeze into clothes that are too small.'

(fullerfigurelifestyles.co.uk)

Big boned

Classic proportions

Well upholstered

*'**Review: Fat Pig starring Kris Marshall & Robert Webb***
On arriving, I was amused to see a large number of well-upholstered ladies in the audience – although it did make me worried for the cast's safety as the Trafalgar Studios aren't very big.'

(Country Life)

Broad in the beam

Having large hips

Wobbly bits

*'**Myleene Klass:***
Mylene, 30, is the bikini body of M&S but she says: "I hate my thighs....all girls have wobbly bits." ...Not girls who earn their living as swimwear models.'

(mirror.co.uk)

Huggable

Overweight

Middle age spread

Weight gain around the waist that happens around middle age

Statuesque

'With a flair for the exotic, Audrey Quock is a male fantasy come true. She defies the norm as a statuesque Asian woman.'

(platinum-celebs.com)

The mature figure

Generally older, larger figures

A generous cut

'Ideal everyday briefs, with a generous cut for the fuller figure.'

Tank ass

Large bottom

Lard bucket

'Pigs, are to this day smeared with sour apple sauce of calumny. They are routinely called fascist, ignorant, stinking filthy swine. Loud actors are hams. Supergrasses squeal. Fat people are lard buckets.'

(timesonline)

A beached whale

Overweight person lying on a beach

Jelly rolls

Surplus fat

Puppy fat

'Some parents are very good at kidding themselves that their overweight child is fine. "It's just puppy fat" is perhaps the most common excuse.'

(The Guardian)

Fashionably thin

'…the health endangering weight loss tactics used by too many women and girls in their efforts to be fashionably thin or meet some unrealistic standard of beauty.'

(clarksvilleonline.com)

A glass of water

A tall, slender person

Lollipop Heads

'Starlets like Mary Kate Olsen, Lindsay Lohan and Nicole Richie have been dubbed "Lollipop Heads" because of their tiny bodies and propensity toward wearing disproportionately large designer sunglasses such as the ones made by Gucci and Marc Jacobs as well as swimmingly oversized "boho" clothing.'

(foxnews.com)

Stick thin

'Kristy Hinze starved herself

"It was the pressure to be really thin that made me work out for 3 hours every day. I'm naturally thin but I'm not naturally stick thin and ended up very sick in hospital."

(Melbourne Herald)

Skinny

*'Nicky Hilton is getting skinny! But the 24 year old heiress calls *** on the rumours.' "There's no truth to any starvation, eating disorder rumours" adding "I think the press has been printing a lot of pictures of me from unflattering angles."*

(flynetonline.com)

Skinny Minnie

'Singer Lily Allen says she was diagnosed with a heart condition about 3 months ago. The Brit, 22 – who dropped from a UK size 12 to size 8 in six weeks – said her sudden weight loss is the result of exercise following the health scare, not because she wanted to be "some Skinny Minnie."

(usmagazine.com)

'I have flabby thighs but fortunately my stomach covers them.'

Joan Rivers

Pregnancy

'You should never say anything to a woman that even remotely suggests you think she's pregnant unless you can see an actual baby emerging from her at that moment.'

Dave Barry

The most special time in a woman's life, a time of joy and anticipation but there are a plethora of phrases used in place of simply 'being pregnant.'

Eating for two

'Ashlee Simpson: Eating for two in New York
While Ashlee Simpson has not yet officially confirmed her pregnancy, she's certainly eating with gusto.'

Expecting

To have a bun in the oven

'Jessica Alba's got a bun in the oven.
Super sexy Jessica Alba and boyfriend Cash Warren are having a baby, her publicist confirmed yesterday.'
(New York Post)

In the pudding club

To be in the club

Up the spout

'Angelina Jolie with seventh child?
Well, well. She's only just dropped and now, if Stateside gossip is reliable, Angelina Jolie is up the spout again.'
(entertainme.excite.co.uk)

To have a baby bump

'Wowsers! Mel C. looks as though she is about to pop! Stepping out with one of the biggest bumps we've ever seen, it looks as though her baby is going to make a bid for freedom at any moment. Is this the biggest baby bump ever?'
(heatworld.com)

In trouble

A dated phrase once used if the pregnancy was unplanned and there appeared to be no husband

To be knocked-up

*'**Knocked-up knock out***
Forget the morning sickness, the leg cramps, the forced sobriety. For an image rebel like me, the excruciating part of being pregnant can be summarized in two words: maternity clothes.'

(The Miami Herald)

In the family way

Up the pole

Up the duff

Ready to pop

'Cate Blanchett is ready to pop
Even though she is ready to pop, she still looks amazingly comfortable – you can see she has that pregnancy "waddle" when she walks'

(theinsider.com)

Cheggars or Preggers

'Billie Piper has been snapped out and about in London… Just days before her first child is due. The preggers star looked very relaxed and calm, ahead of becoming a first time Mum.'

(showbiz.sky.com)

Baggage in the belly

Have a water melon on the vine

In an interesting condition

The Treadmill

'Work is the greatest thing in the world, so we should always save some of it for tomorrow.'

Don Herold

Once upon a time people were loyal to their employers and vice versa. Today however it is a different scenario and we change jobs far more frequently but there is definitely still a stigma attached to being fired.

These phrases are often used when a company is in difficulty and needing to trim down employees.

Bright sizing

Reducing workforce by laying off the brightest workers

Smart sizing

Reducing workforce by laying off the least competent

To streamline the workforce

'Experian Marketing Services has laid off "approximately 130" employees in what it called "a streamlining move."'

(Direct Magazine)

Overhaul of profit margins

The pink slip slump

Negative employee retention

To de-cruit

Productivity Transformation Programme

*'**Schering-Plough Lays off about 50 Research Employees***
"This is part of the productivity transformation programme announced in April 2008", Galpin said.'

(CNN Money.com)

To get the chop

To get the bullet

'Here today, gone tomorrow – but whatever happens to the majority of managers who get the bullet?'

(Givemefootball.com)

To be laid off

To go on eternity leave

Lay-offs

*'**Global tidal wave of 70,000 job cuts***
A tidal wave of lay-offs washed across the world overnight, sending 70,000 workers into joblessness as the pain of the global recession worsened.'

(news.com.au)

A payroll adjustment

To get your marching orders

*'**Job axe fears amid Microsoft rumours***
Speculation was sparked by a report from respected US-based technology blog Fudzilla last Friday, which claimed thousands of workers have been told they will be given their marching orders on Thursday next week.'

(Reading Evening Post)

Having to restructure

'4 Personal computer maker is expected to announce a restructuring plan on Jan 8 that will include layoffs and changes in its top management.'

(Reuters UK)

Having to let people go

A rationalisation of the workforce

An executive culling

'A Conservative government would also conduct a cull of highly paid executives. The Tories are looking at the example of Brentwood Council which removed its chief executive earlier this year and now pays £30,000 to share the chief executive of Essex County Council.'

(Birmingham Post)

To be shown the door

'Time has run out for Hinckley United's Leon Kelly, who has been shown the Marston's Stadium exit door after netting just 2 goals all season.'

(The Hinckley Times)

Dose of P45 medicine

To be relieved of your duties

To take early retirement

'Land Registry forced to lay off 1,200 staff after drop in revenue from fees

All staff over the age of 50 have been offered early retirement and all administrative staff have been invited to apply for voluntary redundancy.'

(Evening Standard)

A workforce imbalance correction

To clear your desk

Irish promotion

...in other words, 'you're fired.'
And then there are the phrases that we use in place of 'unemployed'...

In between jobs

'Henry was spending more time at home now, as he was in between jobs.'

On the beach

An empty desker

Spending more time with the family

'Karl Rove resigning: "The symbolic quit" (for the family's sake).'

(Blogrunner.com)

Transferring to the couch division

In the departure lounge

Resting

Though this is probably only for actors

And those expressions that make the whole issue seem like it was your idea anyway...

To stand down

Not renewing your contract

To relinquish your post

Left to pursue other interests

> ***'Tony Jimenez leaves Newcastle Utd to "pursue other interests"***
> *In a brief statement, the St James' Park club announced that Brixton born Jimenez has quit his role as vice president (player recruitment) in order to "pursue other interests."*
>
> (telegraph.co.uk)

Given new responsibilities

Negotiated departure

Career change opportunity

But here's something that may help if you are in the job market once more and pounding from one job interview to the next…

Body sculpture underwear

> *'Sacked city bankers needing a helping hand to look young and fit at job interviews are among those rushing to buy what is delicately called "body sculpture underwear." It promises to give men a derrière similar to Michelangelo's David.'*
>
> (indiatimes.com)

Or maybe…

The mirdle

'It's for the man who has a little too much of everything – the man girdle or "mirdle."
The stretchy contraptions resemble normal sleeveless tank tops or long sleeved T-shirts only shrunk down two or three sizes.'

(The Canadian Press)

However may be you are one of the lucky ones who receive a financial sweetener on your departure such as….

A golden parachute

'While millions worry about being made redundant, MPs have increased the "golden parachute" payments they will receive when they leave parliament.'

(timesonline.co.uk)

A golden handshake

'Cheshire Building Society savers have attacked the board for its handling of the business – venting anger at a lack of windfall payments, an absence of vote and in particular, a £298,000 golden handshake for chief executive, Karen McCormick.'

(Macclesfield Express)

A platinum handshake

…even better

Or maybe a cash incentive to encourage loyal service…

Golden handcuffs

'Cash for working in tough schools
About 6000 teachers in 500 of the most challenging secondary schools will be offered "golden handcuffs." Inner

city schools have often suffered from high staff turnover and a reliance on temporary teachers – and the proposal suggests a £10,000 loyalty payment in return for 3 years service in the same school.'

(news.bbc.co.uk)

And for the employer, a cash incentive to encourage training for the unemployed…

Golden hello

'At a "jobs summit" in London today, ministers will announce £500m "guarantee" of intensive support to help people out of work for six months back into jobs or training. It includes "golden hellos" of up to £2,250 for employers who recruit and train the unemployed.'

(The Independent)

Gold-plated pensions

'Council leaders should be forced to cut "gold-plate" pensions for town hall staff because they will be unsustainable during a deepening recession, a pressure group said on Friday.'

(uk.reuters.com)

Or if changing jobs there may be some free time in between…

Gardening leave

' "Garden leave" is the term used to describe a situation where an employee is required to stay away from work during their notice period. It is usually used where you have resigned to join a competitor. The employer will not want you in the office speaking to clients and demoralising colleagues.'

(guardian.co.uk)

Money

'Some people get so rich they lose all respect for humanity. That's how rich I want to get'

Rita Rudner

Money, moolah, dosh, dough, loot, it's the root of all evil however we can't live without it and it does apparently, make the world go round.

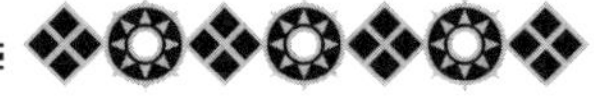

Credit crunch

'Credit crunch victims offered career advice
Careers services are preparing for more visitors as jobs come under threat in Milton Keynes.'

(MK News)

The 'r' word

Rolling re-adjustment

Sustained downturn

'Solicitors jobs in Wigan are the latest to come under threat as a firm announced major cuts following the credit crunch. Ann Harrison, chairman of Stephensons said: "The property market is suffering a sustained downturn and as a result our re-mortgaging work has reduced significantly."

(wigantoday.net)

Go into the red

To be overdrawn

To feel the pinch

'Town centre starts to feel the pinch
The full effects of the economic downturn are beginning to be felt in Falkirk town centre. Regularly named the best town for shopping in Scotland, the High Street is starting to feel the pinch with many mainstays struggling to cope.'

(The Falkirk Herald)

Cash flow problems

Bankruptcy pending

Negative saver

Someone who spends more than they save

Financially embarrassed

Short of money

Deep pockets

'It must be nice to be friends with Tom Cruise, especially as he's got deep pockets. Apparently Tom has his bodyguards carry around stacks of $100 bills so that they can tip random people.'

(theinsider.com)

Filthy rich

'That is what happens when you are surrounded by people who get paid such enormous sums – when you live in the world of the filthy rich.'

(timesonline.co.uk)

Shed load of money

'The good old days when there was a shed load of money coming into the market are gone and people are looking at other alternatives due to falling yields.'

(Sunday Herald)

Meltdown Monday

Mondays with large financial losses suffered by the global markets, followed by….

Turbulent Tuesday

Still suffering financial volatility

Cookie jar accounting

'Hidden by these massive adjustments were their repeated acts of "cookie jar" accounting, where they had shuttled dollars in and out of receivables, reserves and net profit, as necessary to massage their earnings for the benefit of shareholders.'

(seekingalpha.com)

Culture of indebtedness

'Last night opposition politicians blamed Labour for encouraging a "culture of indebtedness" that now threatens to cause an implosion in the housing market.'

(timesonline.co.uk)

Loan Shark

'As a debt owed to a loan shark is not legally enforceable, the lenders frequently resort to violence and intimidation to get their money.'

(thenorthernecho.co.uk)

The never, never

A term used when buying an item on hire purchase, "to purchase on the never, never"

A bung

A backhander

Oiling the wheels

Hush money

A bribe

Queer Street

If a person is 'on Queer Street' they are in financial difficulty

Funny money

'Funny money is now funnier than ever
Once the domain of the criminal elite with access to expensive offset printing presses and ink by the barrel, counterfeiting has become possible for crooks of more humble means.'

(standard.net)

Commercial Clichés

'I couldn't wait for success so I went ahead without it.'

Jonathan Winters

Cash flow issues

'Many potentially sound businesses are at risk – not because they are not profitable, just because of cash flow issues and lack of investment.'

(Eastern Daily Press)

Inconsistencies

Categorical inaccuracies

Disinformation

'But I also mix in some elements of truth and that's the art of disinformation – to mix truths and non-truths in order to confuse people.'

(The Sydney Morning Herald)

Revenue enhancement

Tax

Irregularities

"Irregularities" send firm into liquidation
Printing firm Stewarts of Edinburgh has put the rival it bought less than a month ago into liquidation after uncovering irregularities in the business.'

(The Scotsman)

Chinese bookkeeping

False accounting

Misappropriate the money

Lawyers describing client's theft

Negative growth rate

'The Bank of Japan is close to a decision to downgrade the prospects for the country's economy and forecast negative growth in the next fiscal year due to the global economic slowdown.'

(Thai News Agency, MCOT)

Negative gross profit

Loss

Fiscal stimulus

'No one can be sure if fiscal stimulus will work. We do know that relief for individuals and businesses right away must help more than subsidising a wind farm in 2012.'

(The Wall Street Journal)

Corporate indigestion

'Over acquisition can cause corporate indigestion such as over-leveraging, integration difficulties, cultural misfits etc.'

(businessandlaw.com)

Go into receivership

To go belly-up

To fold

To go to the wall

'Final city Woolies store closes as experts warned of fresh woes

Retail experts predict that the sight of empty shop units in the Capital's city centre will become a more common sight in the next six to twelve months as more chains go to the wall.'

(News.scotsman.com)

To take industrial action

'Scottish Water avoids industrial action after eleventh-hour talks with staff

Last ditch-talks between management and unions averted industrial action by around 1000 staff at Scottish Water. The action, which was due to start at 4pm on Christmas Eve, would have meant workers who normally dealt with water or sewage treatment failures, burst mains or flooding, would have been unavailable over the holiday period.'

(DailyRecord.co.uk)

Asset stripping

'Asset stripping' of cultural treasure

The trustees and governors of the Commonwealth Institute in Kensington, London, are accused of planning to sell off the organisation's prestigious headquarters for millions of pounds and dump its unique 50 year old library on a struggling Bristol museum.'

(guardian.co.uk)

Wildcat strikes

'Teeside workers join wildcat strikes

Up to 300 workers at the Wilton refinery on Teeside joined a wildcat strike yesterday in support of widespread protests over the use of foreign contractors.'

(Journal Live, UK)

Belt tightening

Reduce outgoings

Toxic assets

'The banks have had to use the money simply to stay afloat and they are now counting the cost of their bad debts or "toxic assets" and will be reporting record losses that could sink them.'

(The Herald UK)

Sell at a premium

'Manchester Utd shares sell at a premium
Manchester Utd was shrouded in takeover speculation again yesterday after another large chunk of shares was bought at a high price.'

(guardian.co.uk 2003)

Bottom Fisher

'The Bottom Fisher scan filters the entire market searching for stocks that have traded down for at least 3 consecutive trading sessions and are currently trading higher and signalling that a potential short term bottom might have been found.'

(tonyoz.com)

Incentive compensation

'...he doesn't like to use the word "bonus". "I prefer the phrase incentive compensation."

(timesonline.co.uk)

The feel-good factor

'We need to encourage people to come through the turnstiles and we need to get that feel-good factor around the place again.'

(Walsall Advertiser)

Quantitative easing

'UK Treasury denies report of new money print
The process of printing money to try and refloat an economy is known as "quantitative easing" and was used by the Japanese government as they fought the risk of deflation in the 1990's.'

(FinancialAdvice.co.uk)

Economic pinch

'Community libraries feeling the economic pinch
Traditionally, libraries see an increase in demand for services during tough economic times, especially from job seekers looking to improve resumes and search for employment... "Just how much it may hurt us we don't know. We'll do ok. Librarians are very creative at stretching dollars."

(NBC40.net)

Ambulance chasers

'Pursuing the "ambulance chasers"
The Lord Chancellor, Lord Falconer, is warning firms which encourage people to make frivolous personal injury claims to clean up their act voluntarily or else face tough new regulations.'

(news.bbc.co.uk)

Personal manual database

Calendar

Snail mail

Traditional mail

Dead tree edition

Paper edition of a newspaper or magazine

Aggressive records management

Shredding of vital documents

Flame email

A heated message sent by email, electronic version of the poison pen

Direct mail

Junk mail

Corporate entertainment

'Corporate entertaining is a bit like making the perfect cocktail. One part customer relations, two parts lead generation, a splash of showing off and a generous measure of bonding to finish.'

(The BusinessDesk.com)

Client golf

Level of golf played to avoid defeating the client

BUSINESS BANTER

'My formula for success is, rise early, work late and strike oil.'
Paul Getty

Love them or hate them these absurd phrases have become part of the world of commerce.

Touch base

'Let's touch base next week' - or - I really don't want to talk to you right now

Blue sky thinking

'As the mad scientist of the culinary world, Heston Blumenthal is famous for his bizarre concoctions including snail porridge and mustard ice cream. The struggling Little Chef chain was taken over last year by a group of venture capitalists who probably see a bald, bespectacled chef telling them what to do, in the same way an elephant looks at a mosquito. Boss, Ian Peglar, wanted "blue sky thinking" from Heston, little volcanoes of ideas and imitations of his bonkers ideas.'

(mirror.co.uk)

Cubical warrior

'You'd think that the average white collar "cubical warrior" would be hell bent on actually standing up and moving around when he's not tied down to his office chair.'

Cube farm

Large office separated into cubicles, each person works from their own cubicle.

To source

To get something

Thinking outside the box

'Win by thinking outside the box

I was talking to a woman who has a children's shoe shop and started the business from scratch 5 years ago. Now because of the recession she is looking at having a web-shop. It is looking at different ways to expand your business – you have to look outside the box.'

(The Northern Echo)

Joined up thinking

'For the first time we've got co-ordinated national information for a full journey based on public transport. We've had it before for trains but not for buses and bus timetables are largely a mystery to most of us. This really is the beginning of "joined up" thinking.'

(growupgreen.org.uk)

Guestimates

'The water companies' approach has been to make "guestimates" of surface area using Google Earth and often including permeable, exempt areas such as churchyards.'

(yorkshirepost.co.uk)

To push the needle

Take things up to the next level

To crowd source

To ask people what they think

Let's run it up the flagpole and see if anyone salutes

Present an idea and gauge the reaction

Going forward

We'll do it my way shall we?

Hit the ground running

'But the challenges Afghanistan faces today are already greater than at any time since the Taliban were pushed from power 7 years ago. For that reason it will be critical for Obama and his team to hit the ground running, with comprehensive political, economic and military plans.'

(International Herald Tribune)

To shoot from the hip

Taking action with no forethought

To boil the ocean

A very inefficient way of doing something, i.e. boiling the ocean to produce some salt

Low hanging fruit

Easily achievable

A wrinkle

A problem

Between a rock and a hard place

'The UK government is also in trouble, stuck between a rock and a hard place. On the one hand, markets need financial support, while on the other, government blank cheques are being viewed as disastrous for sterling.'

(property secrets.net)

Out of the loop

Left out of negotiations

Quarterlife crisis

'I don't know about anybody else, but the "quarterlife crisis" is as real as anything for me. I'm 29 with 2 degrees, £20,000 of debt and two part time jobs to pay it off. Neither earns me enough to live on, let alone pay off my debts.'

(timesonline.co.uk)

To network

Gaining connections or contacts for business purposes

Disambiguate

To agree to settle on one meaning for a piece of data

A prehistoric text

An old text

Corridor cruiser

'The ideal user is what Microsoft calls a "corridor cruiser", a manager who is on the go throughout a building or campus with access to a WiFi access point everywhere he or she goes.'

(Techrepublic.com)

Executroid

'Having never built a computer in your sheltered, plush-carpeted, polished-oak executroid lives, you probably don't realise that us computer jocks have soft hands just like you.'

(emperor-norton.com)

To dip your pen in the company ink

'You might have heard the warnings "don't dip your pen in the company ink", but for today's worker that advice is considered outdated. While the office tryst was once viewed as a no-no, society no longer frowns upon a romance that blossoms between colleagues.'

(msn.careerbuilder.co.uk)

A loose cannon

'Is Boris Johnson a loose cannon or a Tory hero?
In the space of 3 days the shadow higher education minister managed to criticise Jamie Oliver's school lunches campaign, suggest packed lunches should be banned and encourage people to use the word "fatso" to describe the overweight.'

(telegraph.co.uk)

Moving the goalposts

'Bradford could have to cope with thousands of new homes on top of the 50,000 that the Government has already said the district must build after Westminster announced it was moving the goalposts on increased housing.'

(thetelegraphand argus.co.uk)

Digital native

A person who has always lived with computers, mobile phones etc

Control freak

'They dominate meetings. They insist on scrutinising everyone's work. They are the first in and the last out. Control freaks exist in every office and are capable of making everyone else's life a misery.'

(management today.co.uk)

Hot button

An important issue

Magic bullet

'There is no magic bullet to combat rising unemployment, closing manufacturing plants and other symptoms of a sick economy.'

(stcatherinesstandard.ca)

Kicking the tyres

'I wanted to kick the tyres and make sure this is real.'

Shelve it for now and we will re-visit at a later stage

This idea/project is going nowhere

Corporate junket

'How to....go on a junket
In the world of work, it's an all-expenses-paid business trip comprising vague objectives and corporate hobnobbing, sweetened with a hefty dollop of booze.'

(guardian.co.uk)

Marketing Speak

'The very first law in advertising is to avoid the concrete promise and cultivate the delightfully vague.'

Bill Cosby

Marketing is a 21st century hackneyed buzz word for 'selling'. We are continually bombarded with increasingly sophisticated techniques that tempt or dupe us whether we are on the high street or browsing through a magazine.

Stock-taking clearance
Factory clearance
Mid-season reduction
Seasonal reduction

A sale

Special purchase

Stock that has been specifically bought to be put in a sale

Premium promotion

Practice used by large chain stores where a charge is levied for merchandise being displayed at the front of store

Special promotional feature

An advertisement

Designer label

'Britain may be going down the tubes, but at least we'll look a million dollars. Natalie Massenet, the queen of internet fashion, is launching a new website selling heavily discounted designer labels as savvy shoppers force down the price of luxury clothes.'

(Sunday Times)

Niche market

'Research last year shows organic farm gate sales rose by more than 80% in the last 4 years – but the organic industry is a niche market and does not have unlimited demand.'

(weeklytimes now.com.au)

KFC

Used to be known as Kentucky fried chicken but needed a marketing facelift so that the word 'fried' no longer appeared in the title, thus moving away from the unhealthy implications.

Fast food

Generally burgers or KFC

Upselling

'Upselling refers to situations where your customer buys a product or service and you encourage them to spend more for additional features or packages.'

(smallbusinesssuccess.biz)

Regular cup of coffee

Standard cup of coffee

'Latte Lingo: Raising a pint at Starbucks
We begin today with a disturbing escalation in the trend of coffee retailers giving stupid names to cup sizes. As you know, this trend began several years ago when Starbucks decided to call its cup sizes "Tall" (meaning "not tall", or "small"), "Grande" (meaning "medium") and "venti" (meaning for all we know "weasel snot").

(itre.cis.upenn.edu)

Guerrilla marketing

'Just 15 years ago, the major ad channels were billboards, radio, television and newspapers. Today, however, guerrilla marketing through a number of social media platforms like "Facebook Inc.," "Twitter Inc.," and even "YouTube LLC" that cost little or no money, are hot.'

(Tampa Bay Business Journal)

Bistro

'Like the Rye locations, this is a convivial, noisy bistro highlighting French and American favourites done up for a contemporary crowd.'

(The Advocate)

Standard rail travel

Once known as 'second class' until that name was abolished in 1987 and replaced with 'standard' however the service remained the same

Weakening consumer confidence

'Consumer confidence dropped to the lowest since at least 2004 in December as rising unemployment rattled shoppers.'

(Bloomberg.com)

Politics

Don't vote for politicians. It just encourages them.'

Billy Connolly

We are all familiar with the patois constantly used by politicians and the media but what do these weasel words really mean?

Political junkie

'For an Australian political junkie at a loose end in the US, nothing could beat working as Clinton's spin doctor.'

(theage.com au)

Political change

A humiliating political defeat

Political posturing

'Despite all the political posturing and huffing and puffing, it is highly unlikely the Government can do anything within the law to claw back or force a reduction in the £693,000-a-year pension granted to former RBS chief executive, the 50-year-old, Sir Fred Goodwin.'

(thisismoney.co.uk)

Flaky

'Gordon Brown has built his budget arithmetic on "flaky" estimates of how much cash he can claw back from closing tax avoidance loopholes, experts claim.'

(guardian.co.uk)

Sexing up

'This is the face the world saw beside Tony Blair for more than a decade, in the shadows at No.10, around Parliament, on the plane. Everywhere. Remember? The world's best known political image-maker, accused of "sexing up" that report on weapons of mass destruction.

(The Sydney Morning Herald on Alastair Campbell)

Dumbing down

A fresh "dumbing down" row has erupted after it emerged universities are awarding record numbers of top degrees.'

Indirect taxation

Stealth tax

'Councils are raking in hundreds of thousands of pounds a years from residents' parking zones. Last night Mark Wallace, campaign director of the Tax Payers Alliance said such schemes had become a "stealth tax".'

(The Northern Echo)

To misspeak

'Washington – Hillary Rodham Clinton's campaign said she "misspoke" when saying last week she had landed under sniper fire during a trip to Bosnia as First Lady in March 1996. She later characterised the episode as a "misstatement" and a "minor blip".'

(msnbc.com)

To cross the floor

When an MP changes political party

Activities incompatible with diplomatic status

Spying

Radical

'There's fear for Obama's safety, concern that he could be assassinated by terrorists or radicals in the south.'

(North Bay Nugget)

Spin

'A decade of spin and error: What a waste of time' John Major 2007

'I am not naïve about politics. Spin – putting a gloss on events – is as old as politics itself... but it's gone too far. Spin today is often downright deceit.'

(timesonline.co.uk)

Spin techniques

Cherry-picking facts to support party's position perhaps sugar-coating the truth

Spin doctor

'Spin doctors at Lambeth Council have been accused of "massaging figures" and "deception" after it released misleading and inaccurate information through its press office.'

(Streatham Guardian)

The Call of Nature

'I wish to report that tiles are missing from the roof of the outside toilet and I think it was bad wind the other night that blew them off.'

Letter to Islington Council Housing Dept.

Even the title of this section is a euphemism! It may be the smallest room in the house but it's positively the most essential and more often than not, when visiting an unfamiliar house or place, we coyly enquire its location in order to "pay a visit".

There is a noticeable male/female divide within this category, although some phrases fall into both camps.

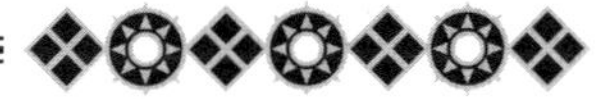

LADIES

The cloakroom

The restroom

'Boston has many wonderful things going for it. Readily visible public restrooms are not among them. We hide most of our facilities away, taunting you, daring you to see if you've got real bladder control.'

(boston-online.com)

I have to powder my nose

"I have to powder my nose" Karen says when we go to a restaurant. "Might as well piss while you're in there," I say.

(indyeastend.com)

I'd like to freshen up
Where is the little girl's room?
A tinkle
Where can I wash my hands?

To spend a penny

> ***'Ryanair customers may pay £1 to spend a penny***
> *Budget airline Ryanair has been criticised after admitting it may begin charging passengers to use the toilet during flights.'*
> (news.sky.com)

GENTLEMEN

Drain the snake
A jimmy riddle
Bleed the lizard
Point Percy at the porcelain
Siphon the python
Test the plumbing
Going to the throne room
Where's the khazi?
Breaking the seal
I need to visit the porcelain god
I have to go to the office to do some paperwork

BOWEL MOVEMENTS

Then there is the matter of 'moving one's bowels' which, if it has to be referred to, make sure it is done in a sensitive, discreet manner otherwise you may find yourself in deep do-do.

Number two

I have to go to the office to do some paperwork

A whoopsie

To do one's business

I'll be making a major transaction

FLATULENCE

Not forgetting, every schoolboy's favourite toilet humour topic, flatulence. Apparently the average human releases 0.5 to 1.5 litres of flatus or 'wind' in up to 25 episodes throughout the day...

A bottom burp or **blast**

> *'We all know that beans are well known as being the food most prone to making your bottom burp.'*

An uncorked symphony

Farticus

Barking spiders

Talking German

Bronx cheer

To step on a frog

'Oops, I stepped on a frog.'

To drop a rose

A butt trumpet

'That Mexican food sure gave me a case of the butt trumpets.'

To break wind

'A rather frank confession by Geri Halliwell.
The singer has admitted she caused a stink on the first meeting with her idol Shirley Bassey – by breaking wind through excitement.'

(ananova.com)

Illness

'Quit worrying about your health. It'll go away.'
Robert Orben

Sometimes people like to give the impression that their illness is perhaps more serious than it really is, particularly if taking a few days sick leave from the office or simply looking for a little bit of sympathy.

Gastric flu

'Crawley skipper Chris Giles was only diagnosed with a potentially fatal ruptured appendix after twice being told he had "gastric 'flu". The same hospital in Bournemouth told Giles that he was suffering from the winter vomiting bug.'
(The Argus)

Funny tummy

Gippy tummy

Problems 'down there'

Problems with the waterworks

Under the weather

'Andy Murray out of Australian Open after five-set defeat against Fernando Verdasco
Murray spent most of Friday in bed, as he tried to overcome a sore head, a sore throat and generally feeling under the weather.'
(telegraph.co.uk)

Man 'flu

'Man'flu is a derogatory term referring to the "snuffles" and mild cold symptoms that a fellow can exaggerate to elicit some sympathy from his nearest and dearest.'

(thisisexeter.co.uk)

Yuppie 'flu

Chronic fatigue syndrome

Migraine

Quite often simply a headache

Dicky, Uncle Dick

Sick, unwell

Heart condition

Used to describe a host of serious heart complaints such as irregular heartbeat, hole in the heart, leaking valve, heart disease and more

Coronary inefficiency

A weak heart

The big 'C'

'For thousands of people diagnosed with cancer every year, sadly contracting the "Big C" isn't the end of the bad news. The few provisions available by the state mean one in seventeen sufferers lose their homes, the average income drop being 50%.'

(Liverpool Daily Post)

STD

'STD's on the rise in South Dakota
The South Dakota Health Department has released its infectious disease report for 2008 and it shows some sexually transmitted diseases peaked at record levels.'

(ksfy.com)

The clap

Byron in Love by Edna O'Brien
'He traversed Europe like a one-man clap epidemic, the nasty thing, leaving a pustulating trail of syphilis and gonorrhea and miserable hearts in his wake.'

An eating disorder

'Fans of Winnie the Pooh are said to be appalled that the return of Winnie the Pooh to the Hundred Acre Wood will include psychological analysis for the bear's "chronic binge eating."

"Pooh is undergoing treatment for an eating disorder related to feelings of low self esteem" explained cognitive therapist, Jim Rouse. "He feels that he is a bear of little brain so he compensates by binging on honey and condensed milk."

(NewsBiscuit)

Chalfonts

Four minute miles

Haemorrhoids - rhyming slang from the town Chalfont St Giles – piles

Social disease

Venereal disease

Kissing disease

'Glandular Fever can be a drawn out and exhausting illness. The infection is caused by the Epstein-Barr virus and is transferred from one person to another through saliva. This is why kissing is one of the commonest ways of catching the disease.'

Burn out

Nervous breakdown

Depression

Corporate anorexia

A business complaint caused by extreme fear of becoming inefficient

TO VOMIT

'Life....is like a grapefruit. It's orange and squishy and has a few pips in it and some folks have half a one for breakfast.'

Douglas Adams

Everybody has experienced at one time or another, that singularly unpleasant occurrence of being sick and although it is most certainly not funny at the time, perhaps the following will raise a smile?

Feed the fish

Sea-sickness

Motion sickness

'Millions of us suffer from travel sickness caused by the motion of aircraft, trains, cars and boats. Relieve the discomfort caused by motion sickness with the anti-nausea wristbands.'

(redsave.com)

Visible burp

Launch lunch

Shoot your supper

Laughing all over your shoes

Laugh at the lawn

Driving the porcelain bus

Worship at the porcelain altar

An out of stomach experience

Re-visit dinner

Eat backwards

Hiccup from hell

Technicolour yawn

'Avoiding the Technicolor Yawn

Astronauts don't talk much about it, but about half of those who fly in space experience Space Adaption Syndrome (SAS) or space sickness, which includes nausea, vertigo, visual illusions and headaches.'

(universetoday.com)

Psychedelic breakfast

Blue chip special

Liquidate your assets

Divulge dinner
Disembarking dinner
Downloading dinner
Spill the groceries
Fling a floor pie
Deliver a pavement pizza

DIARRHOEA

'Diarrhoea waits for no man'

Unknown

There are a variety of terms for this unfortunate state of affairs whether caused by a virus or maybe an unfamiliar meal - and, of course we usually blame it on foreigners! Maybe just steer clear of the shellfish?

Ho Chi Minh quickstep
Mexican two-step
Mexican foxtrot
Delhi Belly
Rangoon runs

Spanish tummy

'The stricken holidaymakers were not just affected by a little Spanish tummy. Norovirus causes acute gastric illness, vomiting and diarrhoea'

(spainforvisitors.com)

Aztec hop
Tokyo trots
Tourist trot
Green apple splatters
Bali belly
Gringo gallop
Lower gastric distress
Butt wrongs

Performance tension diarrhoea

Caused by pre-interview nerves

Montezuma's revenge

'Delhi Belly, Rangoon Runs, Montezuma's Revenge whatever you call it, and there are many names, diarrhoea is the bane of travellers, especially to places where the food and water hygiene is a little suspect.'

(medicine.com.my)

Alcohol

'Will you join me in a glass of wine?'
'You get in first and if there's room enough, I'll join you.'

W.C. Fields

When arranging to meet for a drink with friends it almost goes without saying that alcohol will be involved in a bar or pub, although we never really refer to it as such. There follows a selection of phrases associated with the "demon drink."

What's your tipple?

What's your poison?

What would you like to drink?

Amber fluid

Amber nectar

'The way ahead is amber nectar
Sales of the amber liquid are falling, the cost of raw materials such as barley and hops is rising fast and many pubs across the UK are failing.'

(The Herald)

A jar

A bevy

A sherbet

A swift half

A glass of beer, but not necessarily a half pint

Barley sandwiches

Hop juice

Brewski

More terms for beer

Deep dish olive pie

A martini

Watering hole

'At night I'd have a meal in George St. or at Hadrian's Brasserie in The Balmoral, followed by some drinks in one of the city's watering holes.'

(Edinburgh Evening News)

The nineteenth hole

'Jim Adkins recalled one of the private club's most faithful members coming to just sit at the nineteenth hole for "old time's sake".
"He'd been coming out here for the last 40 years" said Adkins, "he just wanted to sit and have a beer."

(HCNOnline.com)

Wet your whistle

To hit the hooch

Elbow lifting

To lubricate your tonsils

'While the average English fan likes nothing better than a pint or four to lubricate his tonsils and eradicate his sense of perspective before a football match, Italians – especially in the cosmopolitan metropolis of Milan – prefer coffee and conversation.'

(Liverpool Echo)

Hollow legs

The ability to drink a lot of alcohol with very little ill effect

Drinking in stereo

One drink in each hand

Dutch courage

Alcohol induced bravery

Dutch headache

A hangover

To paint the town red

To celebrate, usually involving plenty of alcohol

Boozician

Lager lout

'Interbrew has lambasted UK brewers for pursuing advertising that reinforces stereotypes of beer drinkers as session-drinking lager louts.'

(prweek.com)

A snifter

Smallish drink

One for the road

The final drink of the evening

Giggle juice

Wobbly pop

Any alcoholic beverage

A nightcap

'Perfect nightcap recipe

'To be taken before bedtime. One measure of brandy in a mug. Add sugar and warm milk and a pinch of cinnamon'

INEBRIATED

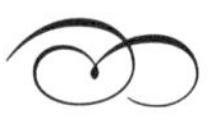

'I can't hold my liquor in the winter.
I'm pretty sure it's the mittens'

Jonathan Katz

The list of euphemisms and dysphemisms relating to drunkenness is lengthy and at times utterly outlandish. Here's the pick of the bunch.

Slightly parboiled

Pleasantly pickled

A little bit merry!!

Somewhat squiffy

> ***'Squiffy Renée Zellweger enjoys George Clooney's post premiere party v.v. much***
> *A red faced Renée had clearly been in the party mood as she was seen looking the worse for wear after the bash at the Automat restaurant in Mayfair.'*
>
> (thisislondon.co.uk)

Totally trollied

> *'The sangria bar was mad – full of trollied people who had been drinking the local brew all evening.'*

Horribly hammered

So scattered

Well-oiled

One over the eight

Rather sizzled

'Eventually they delivered an ultimatum to Gascoigne as he lay, sizzled, in a Portugal hotel: either try to sober up or we can't see you any more.'

(telegraph.co.uk)

Tired and emotional

'Whether looking tired and emotional or outright drunk, in the televisual age there is no escaping public scrutiny.'

(channel4.com)

Absolutely blotto

'Getting blotto is the new motto
British teenagers – girls in particular – now drink more and more often than ever before.'

(telegraph.co.uk)

Quite Jeremied

Moderately mottled

Banjaxed

Utterly legless

'Sexy Coleen is legless
Coleen McLoughlin was spotted looking worse for wear in the early hours yesterday after a night spent knocking back champagne.'

(The Sun)

Half cut

Brahms & Liszt

Fairly Chevy Chased

Pretty leathered

Drunk as a skunk

'...the whiff of alcohol also entices hedgehogs which get as drunk as skunks during all-night binges.'

(guardian.co.uk)

Thoroughly ankled

'No more to drink for me – I am thoroughly ankled – I need to go home.'

Pissed as a newt

'He could play like Hendrix when he was pissed as a newt.'

(theage.com.au)

Nicely Newcastled

'I'm nicely Newcastled but not so drunk that I can't walk.'

Air-locked

Frightfully foggy

Full of loud mouth soup

'A squiffy Taurus will get, er, gregarious (full of loud mouth soup some would say) and is extremely amusing to drag to a karaoke bar when intoxicated.'

(strangecosmos.com)

Got my wobbly boots on

Completely cabbaged

Truly stewed

Rat arsed

'Scousology isn't about quantum theory or the space time continuum, it's about following the Toffees, getting rat arsed and pinching your neighbours stereo.'

(thespoof.com)

Estate Agents

'I want a house that has got over all its troubles. I don't want to spend the rest of my life bringing up a young and inexperienced house.'

Jerome K. Jerome

Buying a home is stressful enough without having to decipher the weird and wonderful Estate Agency language which in itself can be bewildering and baffling.

Property ladder

'..interest rates have fallen twice in the last few months and house price inflation has slowed down, which means that affordability may be increased for the average first time buyer, increasing the chances of getting onto the property ladder.'

(glitec.co.uk)

Property bubble

Over inflated property prices

Up-and-coming area

'In a more turbulent property market, investing in a location that is up-and-coming rather than already popular will give you the biggest return on your investment.'

(upmystreet.com)

Hotspot

'A "hotspot" being a rundown ghetto which will eventually blossom into a desirable area.'

(propertyinvestmentproject.co.uk)

Tight market

Nobody is buying

Bottoming out

'Remember that we will only know that the market has bottomed out when we can see it climbing again.'

(henleystandard.co.uk.)

Bags of potential

Oozing charm and character

Ideal renovation opportunity

Scope for modernisation

A total wreck

Bolthole

'The Bolthole lives up to its name! It's an ideal escape from the world but is also well positioned for the town centre and beach.'

(suffolk-secrets.co.uk)

Bijou pad

'… and soon the sin of envy came to light in the early 2000s, when it became known that all the best people had a flat in Chelsea or South Ken, a bijou pad in Paris, an apartment overlooking Central Park, a frontline (golf) villa in Portugal and a frontline (sea) villa on the Cote D'Azur'

(irishtimes.com)

Pied-à-terre

'This is someone who left the UK and sold property here, but still comes back on holidays and would like to have a foothold here, a nice pied-a-terre.'

(Kansas City Star MO)

High density dwelling

'..the proposed 55 dwellings per hectare, including triple storey flats (total 750 dwellings) are clearly high density.'

(thetimes.co.za)

Development

High volume new build houses, all very similar

Country pile

'Robbie is back for good in a £7 million country pile
Robbie Williams has bought a £7 million country home in Wiltshire. His 18th century home, set in 71 acres has a tennis court, sauna, swimming pool and gym with a large formal garden.'

(thisislondon.co.uk)

Deceptively spacious

'This quaint, deceptively spacious home is located in a quiet secluded neighbourhood.'
Really means a weird, small home

Quirky design

'I appreciate quirky design. The little table made by adding a glass top to an ordinary lamp by Iranian designer, Ali Siahvoshi, brings a new meaning to the idea of a "table lamp."'

(independent.co.uk)

Super prime properties

Properties in excess of £2.5 million

Retro

'..she went a little more retro in the adjacent kitchen with green and beige painted units and a yellow worktop.'

(independent.co.uk)

Urban character

Over-priced dump

Comfort cooling

Air-conditioning

Light and airy

Watch out for draughty sash windows

Fully double glazed

Maybe too close to busy road?

Grey properties

'Grey properties are the ones that live in estate agents' bottom drawers; they're half on the market.'

(telegraph.co.uk)

Brickamortoise

An overpriced house that has been on the market for a long time

Alligator property

Rental property which is now costing more in mortgage payments and bills than it is bringing in for rental. If the situation continues it will eat up all the profit

Due for completion

Nowhere near finished

Distress sale

Property which must be sold due to mounting bills, mortgage arrears

Predator buyers

Buyers who wait and watch for distress sales

Newly re-priced

A price reduction so vendors very keen to sell

Off the beaten track

In the middle of nowhere

Gated community

In a rough area

Easily maintained garden

Small

Mature garden

Overgrown

Rural

Great if you don't mind the farm aroma

Early bird contract

Used by developers to entice purchasers to commit

Clone towns

'The report by the New Economics Foundation (NEF), an independent think-tank, found that 42 per cent of town surveyed were "clone towns" – places stripped of their identity by the global and national chains that have colonised so many of the country's high streets.'

(independent.co.uk)

Doughnut developments

'The doughnut effect is where out-of-town retail leaves town centres void of any serious retail business due to excessive competition. With large out-of-town developments on the cards for Oswestry, the Greens are calling for locals to respond to the planning applications before Oswestry becomes "Shropshire's doughnut."

(westmidlands.greenparty.org.uk)

Lie to buy

Where buyers have been less than truthful in order to get a mortgage

Gazundering

'One of the simplest ways of cutting a deal in a falling market is a technique known as gazundering. This is a sneaky practice that involves the buyer in effect, stitching up the seller by waiting until everybody is ready to exchange contracts, and then lowering the offer on the property.'

(independent.co.uk)

Gazumping

'Yesterday gazumping was once more passing the lips of that endangered species, the estate agent.... The company's Wandsworth branch had seen one buyer try to gazump another by £50,000 after a bidding battle pushed the price on a property from £800,000 to nearly £900,000.'

(guardian.co.uk)

Default landlord

A person who cannot sell so is letting the property

Flipping

'The phenomenon of "flipping" (where an MP claims one house is their second home one minute, and then decides the other one needs doing up and so changes their main residence) has been commonplace in all political parties.'

(walesonline.co.uk)

FTB

First time buyer

LTS

Last time seller (deceased)

'I'm not homophobic. I'm not scared of my house.'

Peter Kay

Families

'Family love is messy, clinging and of an annoying repetitive pattern, like bad wallpaper.'

P.J. O'Rourke

Family is an elastic term that has to stretch to accommodate today's ever changing domestic arrangements. The extended family has reappeared with homes that often encompass more than one generation, maybe for financial or family reasons. The traditional family unit that comprised Mum, Dad and 2.4 children seems to be long gone.

Blended families

Reconsituted families

Jigsaw families

'We are part of that thoroughly modern phenomenon, the "jigsaw family" – a growing number of couples trying to provide a home for our two sets of children, if only for a few days a week.'

(timesonline.co.uk)

Nuclear family

'The phrase "nuclear family" meaning a married man and woman living with their offspring was introduced by anthropologist George Murdock…'

(The New York Times)

Alternative family arrangements

The partners have separated but still live in the same house for family and/or financial reasons

Dysfunctional family

A family where inconsistency and unpredictability is the norm

Pick'n'mix families

'Rise of the pick'n'mix family
Kevin and his wife Pam are the landlord and landlady of the Red Stiletto pub in Vauxhall, south London. Their family consists of Uncle Chris, the DJ, Grandma Betty and the next generation, Colm, Stella and Bernie. The arrangement may sound traditional, but it's a long way from the 2.4 children model. For a start Kevin and Pam are both men. More importantly none of the "family" members are related by blood.'

(bookrags.com)

Parenting deficit

'The problem is that parents are not taking time to show their kids the stuff they themselves grew up in – or wish they'd grown up in, kids are deficient in parents. You might call it "parent deficient disorder".

(worldnetdaily.com)

Breadwinner

"No one is hiring at the moment and, as I'm the main breadwinner, it's very stressful wondering where the rent is coming from."

(The Sentinel, Staffs.& South Cheshire)

Skiing

Spending the Kids' Inheritance

Empty Nesters

'Empty Nesters: how to cope when your children leave home

Mums can feel bereft at home when children go back to college after the holiday.'

(timesonline.co.uk)

Comeback kids

Boomerang kids

'These are young people who find themselves still financially dependent on their parents. I only tell you this to relieve some of the shock should your semi-adult children 'boomerang' back into your nest at just about the time you get used to them being on their own.'

(Pasadena Star News)

Sandwich Generation

Generation caught between bringing-up children and caring for elderly relatives

Kippers

'The so-called KIPPERS (Kids In Parents' Pockets Eroding Retirement Savings) are trapped by financial uncertainty and the cost of housing'

(news.scotsman.com)

Baby Gloomers

'A survey of the Daily Telegraph – the first of its kind since the recession began – highlights the economic burden being forced on to Britain's so-called "baby gloomers" – defined as those who are having to support both their own children and their parents.'

(telegraph.co.uk)

Cabin fever

"I believe in cabin fever, the sense of being trapped in a situation you can't leave."

…when small groups of people have to function in "extreme environments" as in submarines or space shuttles "they tend to get irritable and there's depression", Dr Helmreich said. He added, "I consider being snowed in with kids an extreme environment."

(nytimes.com)

OFFSPRING

'Humans are the only animals that have children on purpose with the exception of guppies, who like to eat theirs.'

P.J. O'Rourke

School days, the best days of your life, just a shame we didn't appreciate them more at the time but, if nothing else, there are always the rather entertaining school reports to look back on....

Mis-spent youth

'People used to say that being good at snooker in later life was a sign of a mis-spent youth.'

(open2.net)

Deferred success

Has failed, but sounds kinder and not so demoralising

Nature Deficit Disorder

Nature Deficit Disorder, in case you haven't heard, is the tendency for modern children to shun outdoor play. They prefer to sit on their rear end and be passively entertained by electronic media (television, DVDs, GameBoys, Nintendo, Computers, whatever.)'

(worldnetdaily.com)

Special education

Remedial education

A keen bean

A diligent student

A swot

'Swots are top of cool class
'Being a swot was once the quickest way to lose friends. Now researchers have found that teenagers who are top of their class are just as popular as athletic "jocks."'

(timesonline.co.uk)

'Sweater, n : garment worn by child when its mother is feeling chilly.'

Ambrose Bierce

SCHOOL REPORTS

Unable to concentrate in class

Disruptive

Has a rather relaxed attitude to learning

Unmotivated

Lazy

Easily distracted

Always messing around in class

Challenging behaviour

Violent tendencies

Has strong opinions

Really quite loud and arrogant

Has a propensity for social interaction

Never stops talking

An under-achiever

A late developer

Not academic in any shape or form

Plenty of room for improvement

Pretty hopeless student

Has education attainment problems

Never going to amount to much

And the usual phrases that emerge every summer when examination results are published…

Grade inflation

'Record numbers of students graduated from university with top degrees last summer, sparking fresh fears over "grade inflation".'

(telegraph.co.uk)

Soft subjects

"Soft subjects", anything with a "studies" in it, as one headmaster remarked, do not win places at a good university.'

(timesonline.co.uk)

Holidays

'I have a large sea-shell collection which I keep scattered on beaches all over the world. Maybe you've seen it?'

Steven Wright

Hurray for holidays! The sacrosanct two weeks every year where we all head off to that little piece of holiday heaven. To laze on a golden beach in tropical climes maybe or perhaps visiting fabulous cities in far-off places or just simply enjoying our own much-loved holiday haunts in blustery Britain.

Boutique hotel

'Move over big boys. Small boutique hotels with special design themes and heritage values are becoming attractions.'

(mysinchew.com)

Boutique festivals

'Standon Calling started in 2001 as a birthday party for about 40 people in the grounds of a 16th century manor house in Hertfordshire. And suddenly it's one of the best "boutique" festivals around.'

(spoonfed.co.uk)

Holiday spirit

Term often used when holidaying in Britain and the weather is cold and raining

Lively

Lots of Irish bars, English pubs, definitely not somewhere to go for a quiet break

Developing/fast expanding

Noisy, dusty with lots of building going on

Ocean view

You may have to stand on a chair though

Just a 10 minute walk from

Could be route march

Bucket-and-spade brigade

'Today I was arriving as a family tourist. One of the bucket-and-spade brigade on a package tour via a charter flight packed full of other Mums and Dads and squirming children.'

(guardian.co.uk)

Bucket shop

Travel agency/airline selling low cost holidays

Clothes optional beaches

'First-timers might find it strange here, even confronting, but the atmosphere is relaxed. The words "letting it all hang out" come to mind. Rolfe frequents nude (or "clothing optional") beaches in summer and nude swimming pool nights in winter. She says a wide variety of people share her passion for living au naturel – from lawyers to hippies to the very straight-laced.'

(smh.com.au)

Extreme camping

'...then there's extreme camping (once known simply as "camping") i.e. climbing Ben Nevis and throwing down a reflective gauze pod that sticks to the ground with suckers.'

(guardian.co.uk)

Extreme sports

Sky surfing, bungee jumping, barefoot water skiing, any sport with a real danger element

Austerity tourism

Using the local cheap public transport

Rave tourists

'20 somethings that frequent the all night clubs'

Leaf peepers

Tourists that come to Britain in the autumn to see seasonal colour changes

TRANSPORT

'Travel is only glamorous in retrospect.'

Paul Theroux

Passenger Transportation Service

A bus

Chelsea tractor

Gas guzzler

'…the previously healthy market for the 4x4 off-road vehicles has virtually collapsed because of the recession. These big gas-guzzlers were popular during the Celtic Tiger years, but people just bought them to try and look cool while they were doing the school run.'

(Herald.ie)

Boy racer

'Bugged by boy racers
Every week I'm overtaken by boy racers showing off. Boy racers testing out their wheels. Boy racers full of testosterone who think they've finally reached manhood now that they've got a car.'

(sundaysun.co.uk)

Safety cameras

Speed cameras

Unplanned landing

Plane crash

The red–eye

'Red Eye Special' does not begin to describe the bleary look of the passengers disembarking from the early morning direct flight to Istanbul from Arbil in the Kurdish north of Iraq. The plane takes off at 4.30am and arrives, after the gain of an hour, at 6.00am.'

(saundayszaman.com)

Jet lag

'I know what it is. I know how it feels. I know there is little I can do to prevent it. But the onset of jet lag is always most unwelcome. That nasty deep down inside exhaustion that makes you space out and wonder where you are, arrives with ferocity.'

(edition.cnn.com)

Open jaw ticket

A ticket that allows you to fly out from one city and back to another

Business class

Club class

More expensive seats on aircraft

Economy class

Tourist class

Cheaper seats on aircraft

Cattle class

Seats at the rear of aircraft

Greenspeak

Enjoy life. This is not a dress rehearsal.'

Unknown

In these days of ecological awareness a whole 'green' vocabulary has evolved and every progressive business or organisation must actively demonstrate its green credentials if it intends to play a part in global ecology.

Greenhouse effect

'Two new studies show that the greenhouse effect is stronger above the North Pole, and that the waters of the Arctic Ocean are acting like a radiator to heat the region's atmosphere.'

(newscientist.com)

Carbon footprint

Measure of the carbon dioxide produced by an organisation or individual

Environmentally friendly

'Mountain View company delivers environmentally friendly diapers that turn into top soil.'

(mercurynews.com)

Green audit

Assessing how much is spent on energy

Green gesture

'Following hard on the Energy Review, Somerset County Council has published its intention to stud all council-owned farmland with wind turbines as a misconceived "green" symbolic gesture.'

(Western Daily Press)

Green gurus

'…well the fact that they are described in the blurb as "green gurus" already sets alarm bells ringing….and all come either from the high-polluting corporate sector or self aggrandising "green" consultancy houses..'

(dofonline.co.uk)

Ethicswash

Greenwash

'Greenwash: Why "clean" coal is the ultimate climate change oxymoron

The people who told us for years that climate change was a myth now say it's all true – but something called "clean coal" can fix it. This is pure and utter greenwash.'

(guardian.co.uk)

Green corridor

'A stone's throw from the busy Newbridge Road is another well-used throughway. But it's not one populated by cars, buses and lorries. The green corridor that runs between Brassmill Lane and Windsor Bridge Road is used by walkers and cyclists – and by children as a play area.'

(thisisbath.co.uk)

Green energy

Energy from a renewable source such as the sun or wind

Eco towns

Where communities live in an environmentally friendly setting with affordable housing

Green collar jobs

'Green-collar jobs "the sexiest around"

He cited examples of such "green-collar jobs": membrane specialists in the water industry, engineers in the solar sector, systems integrators who wire solar panels to buildings, suppliers of sustainable building material.'

(business.asiaone.com)

Green pound

The money spent by ethical consumers on locally sourced, ethically created produce with minimal packaging

Green nappy

'Benefits of "green" nappies

...the county council and district council also held Nappacino Mornings where parents can get a free cup of coffee and talk to other mums and dads about cloth nappies.'

(eveshamjournal.co.uk)

Green deal

'A global green deal

If we're smart, we could make restoring the environment the biggest economic enterprise of our time, a huge source of jobs, profits and poverty alleviation.'

(time.com)

Tree huggers

Ecologists

Bunny hugging

'Shoot saboteurs come in a variety of guises. Although many are vegetarian, bunny hugging, student types, of which about 50% are women.'

(guardian.co.uk)

Eco warriors

'She does make a surprising eco warrior. For a start she doesn't seem like a do-gooder. She's naughty.'

(Style Magazine on Tamsin Omond)

Carborexics

'Dark green "carborexics" – the latest generation of extreme green addicts

Dark green activities in the US include running cars on waste vegetable oil and using one's lawn as a bathroom to save water.'

(zeenews.com)

Ecotistical

A person's inflated views about their own green endeavours

Food miles

How far your food has travelled to reach your plate

Eco icon

'Vote for the bike as eco icon
The Environment Agency is celebrating its 10th anniversary by asking the public to vote for what they believe is the most iconic environmental symbol. The bicycle is on the shortlist.'

(bikeforall.net)

Eco chic

'Using only second hand clothes can Rebecca Simone create a catwalk worthy dress?'

(itvlocal.com)

Grey water

'Grey water – the water left over from dishwashing, bathing and laundry – can form up to 80% of a household's waste water.'

(independentweekly.com.au)

Black water

Waste effluent from toilets

Water footprint

'The average person in the UK (according to Waterwise) directly uses about 150 litres of water per day but behind this direct use there is an indirect use which is about 23 times higher, about 3400 litres per day..... The sum of the direct use and the indirect use is the water footprint.'

(climatechangecorp.com)

Pre-cycling

'...for example purchasing in bulk to reduce packaging or choosing products that can be recycled as opposed to those that can't.'

(canada.com)

Old Age

'They found that the fountain of youth was a mixture of gin and vermouth – let the shaking begin.'

Cole Porter

We often find it difficult to accept old age. The generation that were the 'baby boomers' are now moving ever closer to retirement age, if not already there, with its accompanying wrinkles and health niggles. Once upon a time they were leading the way at the sharp end of fashion but now stylish comfort is the order of the day.

Chronologically gifted

White tops

Senior citizen

'The Senior Citizen, 50 Plus Internet Market is Huge and Growing Fast

The internet habits of the over 50 generation is similar to that of the 18 to 35 age group. However they differ in that they are generally more literate.'

(articlesbase.com)

Silver surfers

Older people who have taken to life online

Coffin dodgers

Bedblockers

A crumbly

A crinkly

A wrinkly

> ***'Patients' tsar slams Government for ageism***
> *He says terms like "crinklies", "crumblies" and "bed blockers" should be outlawed from the workplace in the same way as derogatory racist and sexist words are.'*
>
> (dailymail.co.uk)

Silver fox

> *'Wealthy senior citizens, the so-called "silver foxes", are showing no signs of reining back spending on home improvements despite the economic downturn.'*
>
> (accessmylibrary.com)

No longer in the first flush of youth

> *'World music needs larger-than-life characters, so Daniel Melingo, an Argentine troubadour no longer in the first flush of youth, is a gift. Imagine a proud hybrid of Paulo Conte and Ian Dury, with the facial mannerisms of a silent-film heavy.'*
>
> (guardian.co.uk)

Well preserved

> *'Coolidge had her breakthrough role in the popular comedy "American Pie" (1999) playing a well-preserved, boozed-up Mum who seduces her son's classmate with the admission that she likes her scotch and men the same way: aged 18 years.'*
>
> (movies.yahoo.com)

Woops

Well Off Older People

Woofs

Well Off Older Folk

'The Woofs: a greying generation with golden spending power'

(independent.co.uk)

No spring chicken

Over the hill

Long in the tooth

Baby boomers

'Baby Boomers may have blazed new trails in their teenage years and young adulthood, but they're on track to live out a conventional retirement that looks a lot like that of their parents.'

(Calgary Herald)

Twilight years

Sunset years

'Don't squander away the sunset years
Hooked on the sport of parachuting, former US president, George Bush, is still going strong at an advanced age of 84. When celebrating his 80th birthday in 2004, the former president parachuted from a dazzling height of over 4000 metres, much to the astonishment of the world.'

(mysinchew.com)

Forward at the knees

Alluding to an elderly person's gait

Salt and pepper generation

'Today 50 marks a beginning. It's time to catch up with life, no more worrying about kids, no more work pressures…and the salt and pepper generation are totally living it up.'

(coffeeconversationandmore.blogspot.com)

The blue rinse brigade

'The blue rinse brigade is being replaced by the evergreen shopper – those consumers who want to stay young both physically and emotionally.'

(telegraph.co.uk)

Saga louts

'Bus pass, pension, gold watch… and a comfy chair at "Alcoholics Anonymous".

A new breed of saga louts – retired people who drink too much – has been identified by a top psychiatrist, who claims they are second only to twenty-somethings in their appetite for alcohol.'

(alcoholpolicy.net)

Senior moments

'As I pushed my shopping cart around the grocery store the other day, I almost bumped into a 70 something woman who had just approached a store employee. I could not help hearing her comment: "Young man, I would love to ask you to help me find something, but I can't remember what it is I'm looking for!" She looked self conscious. "I guess I'm just having a senior moment."

(boston.com)

Death

'I'm not afraid of dying I just don't want to be there when it happens'

Spike Milligan

The ultimate taboo, but let's face it, there is nothing more certain than death, it happens to all of us at some time… and nobody gets out alive that's for sure.

The following are the assorted ways that we refer to death… without actually using the 'd' word.

To pass away
To kick the bucket
To bite the dust
To bite the biscuit

If anything should happen to me
To buy a pine condo
To kick the oxygen habit
To leave the building

To pop your clogs
To give up the ghost
To pull the plug

Pushing up the daisies
No longer with us
Gone to meet his maker
The angels have taken him away

A blessed release
To depart this life
To croak
To check out

Gone to the happy hunting ground
The dear departed
Six feet under
To be written out of the script

To be terminally inconvenienced
To fall off the perch
Negative patient-care outcome
A non heart-beating donor

To be astrally harvested
The late John Smith
The fat lady has sung

FUNERALS

'Where would I like my ashes scattered? I don't know. Surprise me.'

Bob Hope

A time for sadness, tears, cherished memories and fond farewells but even funerals do not escape irreverent euphemisms.

Final snoozing place

Grave

Adious park
Headstone park

Graveyard

Wooden box
Pine overcoat
Final bed
Eternity box
Horizontal Hilton
Checked into the wooden Waldorf

Coffin

Funeral director
Grief therapist

Undertaker

Bucket kicking carnival

Funeral

Funeral parlour

Mortuary

Viewing room

Where relatives may say a final goodbye to the deceased in privacy

Garden of rest
Garden of serenity
Garden of remembrance

'The Reigate Garden of Remembrance was designed in 1951 specifically for the placement of cremated remains. This beautiful garden is popular with visitors many of whom frequently return to visit the resting place of their loved ones, to tend memorials, leave flowers or simply to feel comforted.'
(Reigate-banstead.gov.uk)

Remains

The dead body

Floral tribute

Wreath

Obituaries

'May my husband rest in peace till I get there'
Dame Edna Everage

An obituary is, of course, itself a euphemism – the announcement of a person's death. Tributes and obituaries chronicle a person's life cataloguing their triumphs, accomplishments and sometimes their failures. Death can be portrayed as a reward after a good and virtuous life or does the flowery use of language hint at hidden secrets and truths untold?

'the eternity of happiness'
'death is a joyful life'
'to be carried off in the prime of life'
'to be cut away in the bloom of life'
'his loss to society will be long and deeply felt'

Sir Dai Llewellyn (1946-2009)

'A playboy and charming rogue, he was never far from the gossip columns and was dubbed "the seducer of the valleys", owing to a series of amorous conquests. He remained an inveterate party goer.'

(timesonline.co.uk)

Sir Edward Heath (1916-2005)

Michael White writes on Edward Heath:
'To stay in public life for 26 years after being rejected resoundingly by the electorate and one's own party suggests either implacable determination or bloody-minded stubbornness.'

(guardian.co.uk)

Didn't suffer fools gladly

Brusque to the point of rudeness

A man of simple tastes

Vulgar

Fun loving bachelor

Lots of casual relationships

Uncomplicated

Slow

Confirmed bachelor

Homosexual

Tam Paton (1937-2009)

'Behind the fun-filled, facile, fluffy, occasionally inspired, sing-along hits – "Keep On Dancing", "Remember (Sha-La-La)", "Shang-A-Lang", "Bye Bye Baby" – the Bay City Rollers scored in the 1970s, lurked the controversial figure of their controlling manager, Tam Paton. A self-styled svengali, Paton was a bandleader with an eye for the main chance. And, it would later transpire, a penchant for teenage boys.'

(independent.co.uk)

Died suddenly

Committed suicide

Straight shooting personality

No tact whatsoever

Lived a quiet life

A bore

Lived life to the full

He was a convivial fellow
Enjoyed his drink

Fanny Cradock (1909-1994)

'... There was also something sweetly barmy about her clothes. She took to wearing formal frocks and ball gowns (sometimes even a tiara) for her TV demonstrations – looking like a dolled-up socialite who has strayed below stairs to help out in an emergency.'

(Independent.co.uk)

Had a lust for life

Wild

Gave colourful accounts of his exploits

A liar

His door was always open

On a university don - had an eye for the students

An uncompromisingly direct ladies man

A serial groper

Affable and hospitable at every hour

Never saw him without a drink

Uniquely effervescent

A bit crazy

Complex character

A nutter

Ike Turner (1931-2007)

Tina Turner's statement:
'Tina is aware that Ike passed away earlier today. She has not had any contact with him in over 30 years.'

This is definitely an occasion where fewer words have far more impact. Tina Turner spent many unhappy years with Ike Turner as his wife and professional partner during the 1960 – 70's amid stories of a turbulent relationship.

War

Always forgive your enemies. Nothing annoys them so much.'

Oscar Wilde

There is a tendency to wrap up phrases and words associated with warfare and more often than not it is referred to as 'conflict', which has the effect of sounding less harsh and not quite so brutal.

People's militia

'The Burmese military authority has formed people's militias with residents from several villages along the western border in order to act as guards for the border area.'

(narinjara.com)

Military intelligence

Spying

Aerial ordnance

Bomb missiles

Armed confrontation

'An armed confrontation between two Iraqi army units left one soldier and one civilian dead yesterday.'

(Boston Globe)

Special methods of questioning
Refined interrogation techniques
Enhanced interrogation techniques

'In the wake of the Sept. 11 2001 terrorist attacks, hundreds of men identified as members of al-Quaida were captured and imprisoned at Guantanamo Bay, Cuba. There they were subjected to sexual humiliation, sleep deprivation, dehydration, extreme temperatures, waterboarding, being chained to the floor for hours in their own waste, and other so called "enhanced interrogation" techniques.'

(statesmanjournal.com)

Otherwise normally called torture

Pre-emptive strike

Sneak attack

Concentration camps

Civilian prison camps with intolerable conditions

Freedom fighters

'The infamous phrase, "one man's terrorist is another man's freedom fighter" expresses the fact that each side in a war sees themselves as the hero of the story and the other side as the evil enemy.'

(bighollywood.breitbart.com)

Lunatic fringe

The more extreme members of a group

Ethnic cleansing

Displacement and killing of ethnic groups in war situations

Detainee

Political prisoner

Displaced person

Refugee

Casualty

"It's obviously great news that we have all returned safely, but we have taken seven casualties who suffered injuries from shrapnel wounds to being hit by RPG's who will need continuing treatment now we're back".

(hampshirechronicle.co.uk)

Material support

Food, water, shelter

Incontinent ordnance

Collateral damage

'This truly is the season of "collateral damage". As everyone knows, that weasel phrase was coined by the Pentagon to hide the ghastly realities of war, of the killing of innocent civilians and the destruction of their means of living.'

(independent.co.uk)

Soft targets

'Terror raids: "soft targets" might have included nightclubs and shopping centres'

(telegraph.co.uk)

Surgical strikes

'The surgical strike is the seductive dream of people with high-tech weapons at their disposal. Dating from the Vietnam War, the phrase "surgical strike" sounds so efficient, so scientific, so clean. ("We'll just go in there and clear out that bothersome old appendix and you'll be good as new in a day or two.")'

(nytimes.com)

Body count

'Body Count in N.M. Desert No 13
Police said Friday that the remains of two more people have been found during the month-long excavation at a construction site on Albuquerque's West Misa, bringing the total to 13.'

(cbsnews.com)

Dirty bomb

A bomb that will carry on killing and causing harm longer than an ordinary bomb (e.g. by using radioactive materials)

Precision bombing

Bombs aimed at targets of military importance

Friendly fire

"Friendly Fire" Deaths Haunt Families
Soldiers slain by enemy fire are lauded as heroes and honoured with parades. But those who die at the hands of their fellow soldiers in the fog of war don't usually get much attention.'

(abcnews.go.com)

Counter insurgency

Waging war in another country against sections of its own citizens

Holy war

A war caused by religious differences

Permanent pre-hostility

Peace

Department of Defence

Department of War

Deprivation of life

Killing

Hip Phrases

'It's a strange world of language in which skating on thin ice can get you into hot water.'

Franklin P. Jones

Would you class yourself as an 'A' lister or a member of the glamourati? If so you will be extremely familiar with most of these phrases, but for the rest of us who are hopelessly at sea, it is important to know when and where to use these crazy expressions.

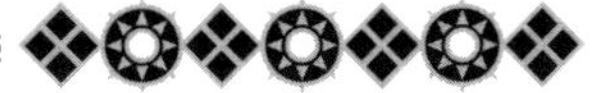

Uber

Kate (Moss) and her boyfriend Jamie Hince, frontman of Uber cool rockers "The Kills", began the evening in a sedate fashion with select morsels of dimsum in the hotel's swanky China Tang Restaurant.'

(mirror.co.uk)

24/7

Available all the time

Pile of pants

Load of rubbish

Estuary English

'Estuary English: Nuffin wrong wiv it?

...and those who adopt the accent as an affectation to get street cred have even got their own nickname – mockneys.'

(news.bbc.co.uk)

Dental spa

Dentist

Café society

Trendy cafés with good coffee, generally patronised by the middle classes

Rom com

Chick lit

'Trashy book amnesty

'I've never read them in public, but on my shelves at home there's a veritable plethora of chick lit, including the entire shopaholic series by Sophie Kinsella.'

(bbcnews.co.uk)

A chick flick

"Nights in Rodanthe" seems to be the ultimate chick flick....at least if the chicks happen to be middle aged or beyond. Near the end of the film, Diane Lane gets to pull out all the stops in a long, teary scene that will almost certainly touch even the most hardened heart.'

(projo.com)

To partner with Revlon

To dye your hair

Retail therapy

'It's going to be an afternoon of fabulously indulgent retail therapy with a unique twist – carefully sourced stallholders with quirky products that are definitely not found on the high street.

(coventrytelegraph.net)

Retail cathedral

'The Mayor of London, Boris Johnson, opened Westfield, a 43 acre shining retail cathedral, to a fanfare yesterday. Europe's biggest urban shopping centre, which encroaches into nine west London postcodes is certainly impressive.'

(independent.co.uk)

A wardrobe malfunction

'Amanda Holden proved she's got a talent for attracting attention last night after almost falling out of her see-through party frock. Thankfully the "Britain's Got Talent" judge managed to narrowly avert the embarrassment of a full-blown wardrobe malfunction in front of the cameras.'

(dailymail.co.uk)

Character lines

Wrinkles

Duvet days

When employees take time off work unofficially

Famocratic

'In our famocratic era, where everyone can be famous for nothing, fame is no longer a meaningful goal.'

(Style Magazine)

Tart fuel

Alcopops

Dry house

Drug rehabilitation centre

Tramp stamp

Arse antler

Tattoo that is on view just above the buttocks when low waist jeans are worn

Social lubricant

'Alcohol is the most widely used social lubricant helping us to relax, reducing our inhibitions and enhancing enjoyment.'

(independent.co.uk)

Disco biscuit

'These are the latest examples of medical slang used as shorthand by a growing number of medics practising in our hospitals. Disco biscuit – otherwise known as the class A drug ecstasy'

(walesonline.co.uk)

Hippie lettuce
Happy leaf

Marijuana

Bling kit

Set of accessories for mobile phone

Flavour of the month

'Coventry City boss is certainly flavour of the month after a superb run of results.'

(Coventry telegraph.net)

Facebook me or **Tweet me**

Contact me via Facebook or Twitter

LOL

Laugh out loud

Mint

Excellent

Plastic words

Meaningless words

Laters

See you later, bye